The
Forgotten
Quebecers

Ronald Rudin

The Forgotten Quebecers

A History of English-Speaking Quebec
1759-1980

1985
Institut québécois de recherche sur la culture

Conception graphique de la couverture: Gilles Caron

ISBN 2-89224-068-9
Dépôt légal: 4ᵉ trimestre 1985 — Bibliothèque nationale du Québec
© Tous droits réservés

Distribution:
Diffusion Prologue Inc.
2975, rue Sartelon, Ville Saint-Laurent
Québec, H4R 1E6 — (514) 332-5860

Institut québécois de recherche sur la culture
93, rue Saint-Pierre, Québec   G1K 4A3 — (418) 643-4695

To Phyllis

TABLE OF CONTENTS

Illustrations

Tables

Maps

Figures

Photographs

Mixed group of immigrants at Quebec City, 1911
(Public Archives of Canada, PA – 10270)

Preface

Historical writing over the past twenty years has seen emerge from the shadows numerous groups of people who had previously been neglected by historians. Workers, women, and a number of ethnic groups have come to occupy a central place in Canadian history, but this elevation in status has not been accorded to the English-speaking Quebecer. When not completely ignored by general texts on Canadian history, he has been presented in the guise of the wealthy businessman living on the flanks of Mt. Royal. In works dedicated more specifically to Quebec history, it is only in the past few years that the term "Quebecer" has been defined broadly enough to include the members of the linguistic minority.[1] To be sure, there are reasons why the English-speaking minority has received such cursory treatment in historical literature. For English and French writers alike, the interest in Quebec came from the fact that it had a French majority, and beginning from this premise the English speaker could barely emerge in any other context than that of the conspicuously wealthy businessman who kept

1. Paul-André Linteau, René Durocher et Jean-Claude Robert, *Histoire du Québec contemporain* (Montreal, 1979), p. 10.

the French down. At the start of the twentieth century, the "Golden Square Mile" of Montreal was populated by a small group of people, most of whom were English speakers, who controlled 70 % of the wealth in Canada. This concentration of wealth and power drew historians' attention away from the fact that these businessmen constituted a numerically insignificant minority within the English-speaking population of Quebec.

This book represents an attempt to provide a broader picture of the English-speaking population of Quebec from the defeat of the French on the Plains of Abraham in 1759 to the 1980 referendum on sovereignty-association. The English speakers to be discussed here were of various religions, ethnic origins, and social classes. In addition, as they settled in various parts of Quebec they came to develop strong regional identities. What these people shared, however, was a common language which frequently drew them together. In an overwhelmingly French-speaking province, this common language led English speakers to share certain institutions, to inhabit certain areas, and, occasionally, to act as a bloc politically.

This work is intended as an introduction to the major trends in the history of the English-speaking population. Many of those trends, which had begun in the late eighteenth century, were reversed roughly at the time of Confederation. Other, newer patterns then emerged and continue to the present. Accordingly, the chapters that follow are largely divided into two parts with 1867 serving as the dividing point. The introductory chapter describes the nature of the various demographic patterns and explains how the term "English-speaking Quebecer" will be employed in this work. While contemporary observers have a wide array of information at their disposal and can use various indices to gauge the size of the English-speaking population, the historian does not have this luxury. The census currently provides two means of estimating the size of the English-speaking population. It gives information regarding the number of Quebecers with English as the language used most often at home as well as the number with English as their mother tongue. Unfortunately for the historian, the information pertaining to the language used in the home is of little use since it has only been made available since the 1971 census. By contrast, complete mother tongue information is available dating back to the 1931 census. Some educated guesswork then makes it possible to estimate the size of the English mother tongue population back to 1759. Throughout this study, English speakers are considered to be those residents of the province with English as their mother tongue.

According to these estimates of its size, the English-speaking population continued to grow as a percentage of the Quebec population roughly up to Confederation. Part I of this study looks at the various ethnic and religious groups that contributed to this growth and describes how the English-speaking population came to be divided by class and regional differences. Special attention is paid to the educational and political systems of Quebec where the divisions within the English-speaking population as well as its interaction with the French majority were particularly visible. In the second part of the study, these same issues are once again addressed, but in the context of the post-confederation period when the English-speaking population continually declined as a percentage of the total number of Quebecers. The concluding chapter takes a look at some of the recent trends within English-speaking Quebec and suggests that a third phase in its history has begun.

This work is a study of broad patterns, and it frequently lacks the detail that would have been available had a substantial literature on the subject already existed. In preparing their much acclaimed *Histoire du Québec contemporain*, Paul-André Linteau, René Durocher and Jean-Claude Robert were able to exploit twenty years of historical research that gave rise to a large number of works, many of which were of the highest quality.[2] This wealth of information unfortunately is not available for the historian of English-speaking Quebec. Accordingly, some subjects, such as the role of women within the English-speaking population, could barely be dealt with because of the absence of sufficient secondary material. This same difficulty has prevented the presentation of a fuller discussion of such issues as the class and regional divisions within that population.

The material presented in this study has largely come from the limited secondary literature that does exist. There are a few works dealing with English-speaking Quebec that are readily available to the public. Donald Creighton's *Empire of the St. Lawrence* and *The English Fact in Quebec* by Sheila Arnopoulos and Dominique Clift fit into this category.[3] More often, however, I was forced to rely upon works such as A.L. Burt's *The Old Province of Quebec*, which dealt with English-speaking Quebec tangentially, or upon studies that exist only in the form of journal articles or theses.[4] The most useful and accessible of these secondary sources can be found in the short bibliographies at the end of each chapter, while the unpublished sources are cited in the footnotes. Moreover, the appendix includes some suggestions for further reading for anyone interested in delving more deeply into the subject. In addition to using secondary sources, a certain amount of primary research was also carried out in the

---

2. *Ibid.*
3. Donald Creighton, *Empire of the St. Lawrence* (Toronto, 1956); Sheila Arnopoulos and Dominique Clift, *The English Fact in Quebec* (Montreal, 1980).
4. A.L. Burt, *The Old Province of Quebec* (Toronto, 1933).

preparation of this study. Most significantly, the census publications issued since the middle of the nineteenth century provided the information for many of the patterns described here. Published government documents were also employed to substantiate my interpretation.

This interpretation might have been given even greater support had I chosen to engage in substantial archival research or had I waited for others to perform this task. For several reasons, however, this introduction to the history of English-speaking Quebec is consciously being presented at this early stage in the research process. First, there is my conviction that English-speaking Quebec needs a strong sense of its past if it is to be in a position to play a constructive role in the life of the province. For instance, the reaction of English-speaking Montrealers to the decline in their numbers during the 1970s might have been less emotional and more constructive had they seen this exodus in the context of others that had preceded it. If one accepts the premise that there is a practical need for English Quebecers to have a sense of their past, then waiting several more decades for further monographs on the English-speaking population to be produced is unsatisfactory. In fact, the second reason for writing this book is that it might generate sufficient interest in the history of English-speaking Quebec to give rise to further research on the topic. Towards this end, the second part of the appendix contains a short list of research projects worth pursuing. If this book should actually stimulate further research, then the day when a more complete overview can be written will be that much closer.

While this work is far from being the final word on the history of English-speaking Quebec, it does attempt to lay out the major issues confronted by this diverse population in the course of over two centuries of history. This task could not have been carried out without help from several quarters. Gary Caldwell of the Institut québécois de recherche sur la culture (IQRC) showed immediate interest in the project when I first suggested it to him several years ago. Throughout the period in which this study took shape, his advice and that of Pierre Anctil, also of the IQRC, proved invaluable. I also owe thanks to Robin Burns and Brendan O'Donnell, who put at my disposal their substantial bibliography on the history of English-speaking Quebec. Charles Bertrand, Dean of Arts and Sciences at Concordia University, did his utmost to provide me with the time to scribble in peace, and my students at Concordia who have taken my course on the history of English-speaking Quebec deserve my thanks for having pushed me to think through my ideas on the subject. This book is dedicated to my favorite English-speaking Quebecer, my wife Phyllis, for reasons too numerous to list here.

I

The Contours
of the English-Speaking Population,
1759-1980

In 1867 most Canadians were considering how the union of the British North American colonies might change their lives. Businessmen looked forward to expanded markets, Ontario's farmers looked to the prairies as a new homeland for sons seeking land, and many French-speaking Quebecers looked with fear at a political system in which they would decidedly be in the minority. English-speaking Quebecers, for their part, tried to calculate how their interests would be affected by the creation of the overwhelmingly French province of Quebec. However, what few English speakers could have realized in the 1860s was that their population was in the process of undergoing some very basic changes which were unrelated to Confederation. These changes, in the long run, would influence their history more than any political change that was then taking place.

In 1867 English-speaking Quebecers were in no position to know that their share of the population of the province would thereafter steadily decline. While nearly 25 % of all Quebecers were English speakers in 1867, this figure fell without interruption until the 1981 census gave that population only 11 % of the Quebec total.[1] Similarly, at Confederation English speakers, nearly all of whom could trace their roots back to Great Britain, could not have predicted that in the post-1867 era their population would increasingly be made up of people from places such as Russia and Italy. In the 1860s English Quebecers professed either Catholicism or some form of Protestantism in terms of religious belief, but in the post-confederation era Jews and other religious groups were added to the picture. Finally, English Quebecers in 1867 could scarcely imagine the changes that lay ahead in terms of the regional distribution of their numbers. At the time of Confederation the single largest regional concentration of English speakers was to be found in the Eastern Townships, but during the period after 1867 most areas outside of Montreal witnessed a decline in their English-speaking populations, while Montreal itself became the home of roughly three-quarters of all English Quebecers.

These demographic changes have altered all aspects of English-Quebec life and have influenced the relationship of that population with Quebec's French-speaking majority. At the time of Confederation, to take only one example, certain leaders of the English population were able to secure concessions for this group not only because of their considerable economic influence but also owing to the demographic strength of the population they claimed to represent. They were able to make certain demands, secure in the knowledge that the English population made up a significant and, up to then, ever-growing percentage of the population of Quebec. Their case was strengthened by the fact that the English population was prominent not only in Montreal, but also in the Eastern Townships

---

1. All population data in this study, both in the text and in the tables, are derived from the Canadian census, unless otherwise indicated.

and the Ottawa Valley. By contrast, English Quebec's leaders in the 1980s bargained from a much weaker position in the light of a population in decline in terms of both its absolute numbers and its relative place within Quebec. Their case was further compromised by the increasing ethnic diversity of this population and its perilous existence outside of Montreal.

The purpose of this introductory chapter is to sketch out these demographic changes in the broadest of strokes. Subsequent chapters will describe in greater detail the various groups that have made up English-speaking Quebec. The interest here is in charting the general trends in the evolution of that population with a particular emphasis upon Confederation as the point in history at which certain changes began to take place.

1.   The Size of the English-Speaking Population

How many English speakers lived in Quebec in 1781, or 1881, or even 1981? As straightforward as this question might appear, it is not easily answered. To do so, one needs both a definition of who qualifies as an English speaker and the data to provide reliable figures to satisfy that definition across two hundred years of history. The 1981 census offers data for two possible definitions. First, it tells us that there were 809,145 Quebecers who identified English as the language they used most often at home. In addition, we learn that 706,115 Quebecers claimed English as their mother tongue. Of the two, the former provides the better definition of an English-speaking Quebecer. The mother tongue information tells us the number of people with English as the language first learned and still understood, but the home language information includes a further 100,000 people who came to adopt English as their primary language of communication in the home but who did not have English as their mother tongue.

The problem with employing home language as the gauge for estimating the size of the English-speaking population over time is that this classification does not exist prior to the 1971 census. By contrast, mother tongue information for the entire population was first presented in the 1931 census. Accordingly, for the sake of consistency in the data presented the mother tongue definition will be employed. Throughout this study, an English-speaking Quebecer will be thought of as a person with English as his mother tongue.

Even this definition is not without its problems, however. Prior to 1931 there is no information regarding the mother tongue of the population. This problem is not insurmountable, however, given the nature of the evolution of the English-speaking population. Prior to the beginning of the twentieth century, the vast majority of the non-French population of Quebec was of British origin. According to the census taker, one's ethnic origin was determined through the paternal line and was defined by the country from which that side of the family first came to North America. In 1901 nearly 90 % of the Quebec population that was not of French origin could trace its roots back to England, Scotland or Ireland, a figure that was even higher in the last decades of the 1800s. In the first decades of the twentieth century, other ethnic groups began to arrive in Quebec in large numbers, but as late as 1931 relatively few of the members of these groups had adopted English as their mother tongue. Jews made up the most important group among these newcomers, but in 1931 only 252 out of 60,000 had English as their mother tongue. Accordingly, as late as 1931 there was still a certain logic to equating the English mother tongue population with that which was of British origin. Indeed, the 1931 census listed 432,726 Quebecers as being of British origin and 429,613 as having English as their mother tongue. [2]

Although it is possible to use the British origin population as a surrogate for those with English as their mother tongue in the censuses from 1871 to 1921, prior to Confederation there are other problems to tackle. Between 1760 and 1844, for instance, censuses were held only intermittently. The information that was collected regarding the ethnicity of the population was regarded by one historian as "inconsistent", and to make matters worse the early governors of Quebec were not beyond falsifying the records to serve their own purpose. [3] With the census of 1851, the system took on a certain regularity as, from that point on, censuses were to be held on a decennial basis. Even so, the censuses of 1851 and 1861 do not provide clear information regarding the size of the British origin population. Accordingly, throughout the pre-Confederation period one has to rely upon figures that pertain to the non-French population of Quebec. Once more, however, this assumption is fairly safe given the fact that in 1871 93 % of the Quebec population not of French origin claimed to have been of British origin. Based upon all of these various assumptions, the following table presents estimates of the size of the English-speaking population from the Conquest to 1981.

2. The British figure is higher owing to the existence of many Quebecers of British origin who had French as their mother tongue in 1931.

3. Fernand Ouellet, *Lower Canada, 1791-1840* (Toronto, 1980), p. 107; Ouellet, *Economic and Social History of Quebec* (Ottawa, 1980), pp. 149-150.

TABLE 1.1

The Size of the English-Speaking Population, 1766-1981

YEAR	NUMBER OF ENGLISH SPEAKERS	% OF THE TOTAL POPULATION OF QUEBEC	CRITERION EMPLOYED
1766	500	1	Non-French origin
1780	2,000	2	"
1792	10,000	6	"
1812	30,000	10	"
1827	80,000	16	"
1844	172,840	25	"
1851	220,733	25	"
1861	263,344	24	"
1871	243,041	20	British origin
1881	260,538	19	"
1891	N/A	N/A	Data regarding origins not produced
1901	289,680	18	British origin
1911	318,799	16	"
1921	356,943	15	"
1931	429,613	15	English mother tongue
1941	468,996	14	"
1951	558,256	14	"
1961	697,402	13	"
1971	789,175	12	"
1981	706,115	11	"

Source: Fernand Ouellet, *Economic and Social History of Quebec* (Ottawa, 1980), p. 659; *Census of Canada,* 1844-1981.

What these estimates indicate is that up to the 1850s English speakers made up an ever-growing percentage of the population of Quebec. Then, beginning most strikingly in the decade of Confederation, the percentage began to decline, and it continued to do so up to the start of the 1980s. In the decade of the 1970s the decline in the English-speaking population was not only a relative one, but also an absolute one. This was not, however, the first decade to have recorded such an absolute reduction. Between 1861 and 1871 there was a decline in the number of English speakers of 20,000, and this was not simply a function of switching from one criterion to another as there was also an absolute decline in the number of non-francophone Quebecers. The 1860s therefore provided a sneak preview of the demographic history of English-speaking Quebec in the post-Confederation era.

By that decade the waves of immigrants from Britain and the United States that had steadily bolstered the relative position of the English-speaking population had largely subsided. This was apparent in the "Canadianization" of Quebec's non-French population in the two decades leading up to Confederation. In 1844 only half of this population was born in Canada, a figure that reached 65 % by 1861 and 73 % by 1871. At the same time as the flow of newcomers dried up, there was a significant movement of English speakers from the province during the 1860s, particularly from the Quebec City region which was experiencing profound economic changes. This movement of English speakers in search of better economic prospects outside Quebec was to be a major factor in the relative decline of this population throughout the post-Confederation period. English speakers regularly took advantage of the fact that they, unlike their French-speaking counterparts, could easily move to other parts of North America without having to make any linguistic adjustment.

Throughout the history of Quebec there was only one major movement of French speakers outside the boundaries of the province. During the second half of the nineteenth century, hundreds of thousands of French speakers moved to New England to take up jobs in the region's textile mills. [4] New England had the attraction of proximity to Quebec that made returning to the province a relatively simple proposition and reduced fears of assimilation. However, when it came to moving farther away from the province there was a decided lack of enthusiasm on the part of French speakers. This was particularly the case when the Canadian prairies were opened up for settlement towards the end of the 1800s. [5] Having thus restricted their options, when the need for employees in the New England mills ended towards the turn of the century, there was no further significant movement of French speakers from the province. Less concerned about straying from Quebec, English speakers regularly left when better economic prospects presented themselves elsewhere on the continent.

Up until the late 1970s this outward movement of English speakers was counterbalanced by three factors: the arrival of English speakers from outside the province, the natural growth of the resident English-speaking population, and the actions of Quebecers whose mother tongue was not English but who passed English along as the mother tongue of their children. Between 1971 and 1976 the last two of these factors made it possible for the English-speaking population to increase by 11,000 in spite of a net loss to other provinces of 50,000. During the second half of the

---

4. Gilles Paquet, "L'émigration vers la Nouvelle Angleterre", *Recherches sociographiques*, V (1964), pp. 319-370.

5. Arthur Silver, "French Canada and the Prairie Frontier, 1870-1890", *Canadian Historical Review*, L (1969), pp. 11-36.

1970s, however, nothing could prevent an absolute decline in the English-speaking population. Between 1976 and 1981 there was a decline of roughly 95,000 in the number of English speakers, largely due to the net loss to other provinces of 106,000 people. Political fears engendered by the rise to power of the Parti Québécois combined with the economic factors that had always encouraged English speakers to pack their bags. Moreover, the environment of the late 1970s did little to encourage those whose mother tongue was not English to pass that language along to their children. With few new recruits to bolster its ranks and with many of its numbers leaving the province, English-speaking Quebec faced a situation in the 1970s that echoed some aspects of the decline of the 1860s. These two decades shared many of the trends of the post-Confederation period, which were markedly different from those of the period prior to 1867.

2. Ethnicity, Religion and Race

At the time of Confederation there was a certain uniformity in the ethnic, religious and racial makeup of the English-speaking population. In terms of ethnic origin, nearly all Quebecers who were not French Canadians could trace their roots back to Britain. Nearly half of these Quebecers of British origin were Irish, followed by the English and then the Scots. As for the religion of most English speakers, one can safely say that they were Christians since fewer than 1,000 non-Christians lived in the province in 1871, most notably Jews who numbered 549. One should not, of course, minimize the divisions between Protestants belonging to different denominations as well as those between Protestants and Catholics. In the same sense, the divisions between the different "British" nationalities cannot be ignored. Finally, in terms of race, nearly all

English speakers were white since there were only 148 Quebecers of "African" origin in 1871, while the various Oriental nationalities were not even listed in the census.

While this relatively straightforward situation came to an end during the post-Confederation period, little change actually occurred until after the turn of the century. The percentage of all non-French Canadians who were of British origin only fell from 93 % in 1871 to 89 % in 1901. However, with the advent of the new century and the arrival of large numbers of Jews and Italians, the simplicity of nineteenth century Quebec disappeared. By 1931 these two groups accounted for 85,000 Quebecers, but few Jews and Italians had yet claimed English as their mother tongue. In that year 95 % of those with English as their mother tongue were of British origin, but as Table 1.2 indicates this situation changed greatly in the following half century.

TABLE 1.2

**English Speakers of British Origin,
1931-1981**

Year	% OF QUEBEC ENGLISH MOTHER TONGUE POPULATION OF BRITISH ORIGIN
1931	95 %
1941	89
1951	80
1961	73
1971	67
1981	60

Source: *Census of Canada.*

For the Jews, the most numerous of the pre-depression immigrants, successive generations over-whelmingly came to adopt English as their mother tongue. Of 60,000 Jews in 1931 only 252 had English as their mother tongue. This last figure had increased to 73,000 by 1971 out of a total Jewish population of 116,000. As for the Italians, by 1971 nearly 15,000 of their number had English as their mother tongue as opposed to 725 in 1931. A further 10,000 spoke English most often at home and were likely to pass that language on to the next generation. Between 1931 and 1981 Quebecers of French origin also rapidly moved into the English stream as the number within that group having English as their mother tongue grew from 12,000 to slightly over 100,000. At the same time the British element grew slowly, and in the exodus of the 1970s the number of English speakers of British origin actually declined by 21 %.

These various changes resulted in the dissolution of ethnic, religious and racial uniformity within the English-speaking population. By 1981, 40 % of this population was of various non-British origins, while nearly 10 % was Jewish.[6] As for the racial composition of the English-speaking population, one has to be cautious because of severe limitations in the available data. Nonetheless, a conservative estimate would place the number of English-speaking Blacks and Orientals at 20,000 in 1981, once again because of twentieth century immigration.[7]

---

6. The 1981 census presents certain problems in terms of the use of the ethnic origin information. While previous censuses asked respondents to define their ethnicity through their paternal line, the 1981 census gave them the possibility of taking their mother's ancestry, if different, into account by declaring multiple origins. Whenever possible, the 1981 data have been adjusted to make them comparable to information from earlier censuses.

7. On this issue, see Chapter VI for more detail.

3. Regional Distribution
of the English-speaking Population

At the time of Confederation the single largest regional concentration of English speakers was located in the Eastern Townships. In 1861 only one-quarter of the English-speaking population lived in the Montreal region while over two-thirds lived in either the Eastern Townships, the Ottawa Valley, the Gaspé, or the region of Quebec City.[8] In all of these regions the pre-Confederation period was marked by a large percent-

---

8. Throughout this text references will be made to five different regions: Montreal, Quebec City, the Ottawa Valley, the Eastern Townships and the Gaspé. It is obviously essential that these regions be defined in a consistent manner across the period under study so as to present meaningful comparisons. This can create some difficulties as the size of the Montreal region has grown over time under the influence of urban sprawl. In their book, *The Demolinguistic Situation in Canada*, Réjean Lachapelle and Jacques Henripin have defined the Montreal region very broadly to include large sections of the Eastern Townships. While this might seem reasonable in terms of the situation in the late twentieth century, such a definition cannot be applied to the nineteenth century without giving a false impression of the English-speaking population in the Eastern Townships.

In this text the Montreal region has been defined in a more limited manner so that the existence of important English-speaking populations outside the metropolitan area can easily be perceived. At the same time, Huntingdon County in southwestern Quebec has been added to the Eastern Townships even though that region normally does not extend west of the Richelieu River. This extension was seen as reasonable given the similar histories of the English-speaking populations on both sides of the Richelieu.

The regions discussed in this text were consistently defined as encompassing the following counties:

1) *Montreal region*: Island of Montreal, Île Jésus, Chambly, Laprairie, Beauharnois, Châteauguay, Deux-Montagnes, Vaudreuil, Soulanges.

2) *Quebec City region*: Quebec City, Quebec County.

3) *Ottawa Valley*: Gatineau, Hull, Labelle, Papineau, Pontiac, Argenteuil.

4) *Eastern Townships*: Compton, Frontenac, Richmond, Sherbrooke, Stanstead, Wolfe, Megantic, Shefford, Brome, Drummond, Arthabaska, Missisquoi, Huntingdon.

5) *Gaspé*: Gaspé, Bonaventure, Matane, Matapédia, Rimouski.

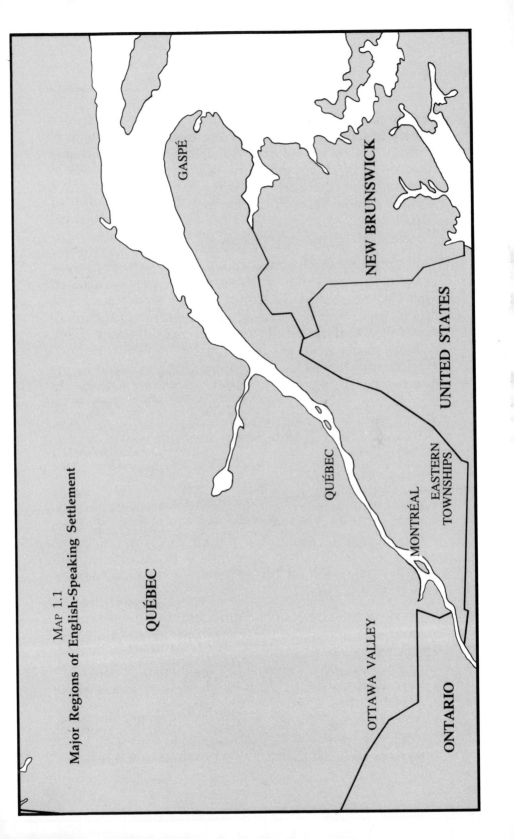

Map 1.1
Major Regions of English-Speaking Settlement

age of English speakers in the total regional popula-
tion. For instance, in the city of Montreal there was an
English-speaking majority in 1861, while in Quebec
City 44 % of the population was English-speaking in
that year. In the rural regions, English-speaking ma-
jorities existed in both the Eastern Townships and the
Ottawa Valley, while 25 % of the residents of the
Gaspé were English speakers in 1861.

Throughout the pre-Confederation period English
speakers in each region fashioned lives for themselves
that differed markedly from those of their co-linguists
in other parts of Quebec. This was partly a function of
the origins of those who settled the different areas.
While people who had been loyal to the British crown
during the American Revolution came to settle in the
Gaspé region, Americans, some of whom had fought
against the British in the revolution, came to open up
the Eastern Townships and the Ottawa Valley between
1792 and 1812. There were also differences in the
economic base of each region that contributed to the
regional divisions within the English-speaking population. Fishing was the basis for survival in the Gaspé,
while farming was essential to the Townshippers, as
was the lumber industry to residents of the Ottawa
Valley. Finally, the limited nature of communications
and transportation facilities in the pre-Confederation
period further added to the sense of regional identification that existed.

During the decade of Confederation, however, the
strength of several of these concentrations of English
speakers began to show evidence of decline. During
the 1860s the English-speaking population of the Eastern Townships fell by 13 % while that of Quebec City
was reduced by 10 %. This process of absolute decline,
with few exceptions, continued for the English-
speaking population outside Montreal throughout the
post-Confederation period. The immigrants who came

to Quebec in the twentieth century invariably settled in Montreal, thus further contributing to the steady growth in the concentration of the English-speaking population in Montreal that is evident in Figure 1.1. The concentration of English speakers in the province's metropolis was always far greater than was the case for the population of Quebec in general.

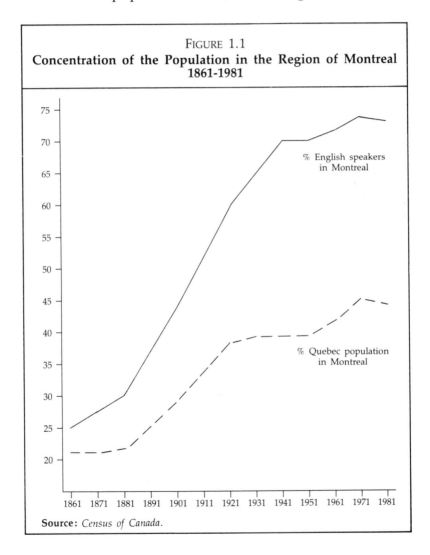

FIGURE 1.1

Concentration of the Population in the Region of Montreal 1861-1981

% English speakers in Montreal

% Quebec population in Montreal

Source: *Census of Canada.*

For those English speakers who continued to live in the areas outside of metropolitan Montreal, there were numerous difficulties that had not been experienced in the pre-Confederation period. In the Eastern Townships, for instance, where two-thirds of the population had been English-speaking in the 1840s, it had been possible to crown the local educational system with a university, for Bishop's was established in that decade. However, as English-speaking people moved out with their place largely taken by French speakers, the ability to support English-speaking institutions was thrown into doubt. There were, therefore, two demographic changes striking areas such as the Townships throughout the post-Confederation period. In addition to the decline of the English-speaking population of the region as a percentage of all English speakers, there was also the precipitous decline of the English-speaking population of the region as a percentage of that region's total population. In eight Quebec counties the majority of the population was English-speaking in 1871, but by 1961 only Brome and Pontiac counties had such majorities, and by 1981 only Pontiac remained.

4. Conclusion

Not all of the demographic issues of importance to the history of English-speaking Quebec have been presented in this chapter. Issues such as the age structure of the population have not been raised, but will be examined in greater detail in subsequent chapters. The point here has been to provide an introduction to some of the most important demographic trends which can be traced back to the pre-Confederation period. In so doing, we have seen that there were certain patterns in the history of the English-speaking population up to 1867 that were reversed in the years that followed. Prior to Confederation the English-speaking population continually grew as a percentage of the total population of Quebec, while after 1867 this percentage declined. The English-speaking population was overwhelmingly of British origin and dispersed across the province at the time of Confederation, but in the post-1867 period ethnic diversity came to be the rule as did the concentration of the population in Montreal. To elaborate upon these patterns, the chapters that follow are divided into two parts with Confederation as the watershed.

SELECT BIBLIOGRAPHY

Caldwell, Gary. *A Demographic Profile of the English-Speaking Population of Quebec, 1921-71*. Quebec, 1974.

Caldwell, Gary and Eric Waddell, eds. *The English of Quebec: From Majority to Minority Status*. Quebec, 1982.

Charbonneau, Hubert et Robert Maheu. *Les aspects démographiques de la question linguistique*. Quebec, 1973.

Lachapelle, Réjean and Jacques Henripin. *The Demolinguistic Situation in Canada*. Montreal, 1982.

Ouellet, Fernand. *Economic and Social History of Quebec, 1760-1850*. Ottawa, 1980.

PART I

Conquest to Confederation, 1759-1867

During the century leading up to Confederation English-speaking Quebec grew from a negligible population to one with nearly a quarter of a million people in its ranks. These people shared both a common language and a common heritage as nearly all of them could trace their roots back to Great Britain. Nevertheless, there were various ethnic streams within this British population, and further divisions emerged based upon religious, regional and class identities. There were certain moments at which English speakers put these differences aside and spoke with a single voice on political matters, but more common were those situations in which different and often conflicting claims were advanced by the various segments of the population. Because some groups within this population were significantly stronger than others, several of them were sufficiently influential in 1867 to have their interests recognized in the British North America Act.

II

The Foundations
of English-Speaking Quebec

The first English-speaking Quebecers arrived well
before the army of General Wolfe in 1759. Irishmen
such as Jean LaHaye (né Leahy) arrived in Quebec in
1693, and Timothy Silvain (né Sullivan), a doctor,
made the trek in the early eighteenth century.[1] In
addition, one researcher has found that there were at
least 500 Protestants in the French colony along the St.
Lawrence, many of whom came from Scotland. Scotland had long had ties with France, and there is
evidence that a Scottish Protestant sailed to Canada
with Champlain in 1618.[2] But the most noteworthy of
these Scots was one Abraham Martin, dit l'Ecossais.
One can only assume that the suffix was added so as
to signify his ethnic origin. Martin was such a noted
pilot in New France that the Plains of Abraham were
named after him. It is ironic that the British took
control of Quebec on real estate named after a Scottish
immigrant.

---

1. Thomas Guérin, *The Gael in New France* (Montreal, 1946).
2. Marc-André Bédard, *Les protestants en Nouvelle-France* (Quebec, 1978);
   Henry Best, "The Scot in New France During the Old Regime," M.A.
   Thesis, Université Laval, 1957; W. Stanford Reid, *The Scottish Tradition in Canada* (Toronto, 1976).

These pre-conquest English speakers[3] have a certain curiosity value, but they were never sufficiently numerous to form a community, nor were there any institutions explicitly designed to serve their needs. They simply became French colonists of British origin. It was not until after 1760 and the end of French colonial rule that this situation changed. By 1867 over a quarter of a million English-speaking people, almost all of British origin, had established themselves in Quebec, and this number does not include all those English speakers who resided in Quebec for a time before moving on to other parts of North America. Those who were living in Quebec at the time of Confederation were divided by ethnic, religious, and class distinctions. They also were divided by their attachment to the regions where they settled and by the particular circumstances under which they came to Quebec. To better understand those circumstances, this chapter is organized chronologically according to the four major waves of English-speaking immigration that occurred prior to Confederation. Not all English speakers who arrived before 1867 fit into one of these categories, but the overwhelming majority did belong to one of these groups. By concentrating upon these various streams of immigrants, it is possible to gain a firm sense of the different elements within the English-speaking population.

---

3. One of the unanswerable questions regarding the history of English-speaking Quebec is determining the number who had Gaelic as their mother tongue. In the absence of any useful data on this issue, the assumption here is that all pre-Confederation immigrants from Britain came to Quebec capable of speaking English even if some of them might not have had English as their mother tongue.

1. The Camp Followers

Following the military defeat of France in 1760, British colonial officials anxiously looked forward to a substantial immigration of British subjects, particularly from the American colonies to the south. While the British were in no position to facilitate this movement prior to the formal ceding of the territory in 1763, as soon as the transfer took place they acted to resolve the difficulties of ruling a French majority by encouraging English speakers to come to the colony in order to reduce this French majority to a minority.

The plans of the British for Quebec were spelled out in the Proclamation of 1763. By imposing British laws and British political institutions upon Quebec, the colonial officials hoped to create an English-speaking majority. For instance, by establishing British law regarding property, the seigneurial system of land holding which had been in place since the 1600s was technically suppressed. In this sytem, which had at least the appearance of feudalism, the individual farmer occupied the role of a tenant who owed various fees to his lord, the seigneur. British subjects, particularly those in New England who had farmed land that was their property under a system of free and common soccage, were hardly going to be induced to emigrate only to come under the French system of landholding. By imposing the British system, the way was clear, or so colonial officials thought, for a considerable influx of English speakers. The French might complain, but if they were forced into a minority situation their complaints could easily be ignored. British officials were so confident that waves of New England farmers were on their way that they even prepared plans to survey the land into square townships, along the lines that then existed in New England, and in opposition to the French custom of laying out long rectangular strips extending back from a river or a stream. As historian

A.L. Burt has noted, "All this [had] a clear and unmistakable meaning. The home government was anticipating a large influx of population from the south."[4]

In expectation of the arrival of these immigrants the Proclamation of 1763 also provided for the establishment of an elected assembly to rule the colony. At this time Catholics were barred from voting or holding office under British law, which meant that only the newcomers were going to be able to participate in the political process. Proposing such a system would have made no sense had the British believed that the French-Catholic population was to remain the majority. These rules were established to facilitate the British migration, which was believed to be just over the horizon, and which would soon contribute to an English-speaking majority. The assumption that this new majority was imminent was not unfounded in 1763. After all, there were only 60,000 habitants living in the French colony along the St. Lawrence, while there were more than a million people living in the American colonies to the south. Surely, given the right circumstances, a small percentage of them would come to Quebec and its abundant land.

Had this influx materialized the whole course of Canadian history would have been altered; but the hoped-for migration of New England farmers never occurred. Apparently, the British miscalculated the severity of the demographic pressures upon the land to the south in the early 1760s. But while the farmers did not emerge upon the Quebec scene, another group of English speakers did arrive, a collection of merchants and traders that some have unkindly described as camp followers.

In an age before the British army had its own services to provide supplies, independent merchants

---

4. Burt, p. 82.

would follow the camps of these armies around the world to see that their needs were looked after. Not surprisingly, if the British army was successful in whatever campaign it was involved in, these merchants would be in an ideal position to remain on the spot and assume the trade of the conquered territory; and this is precisely what occurred in Quebec. Approximately one hundred such merchants stayed in Quebec City during the winter of 1759-60, and still others came with the arrival of further troops after the final fall of New France in 1760. While most of these merchants had ties with British commercial houses, there were also some who came from the colonies to the south. This part of the burgeoning merchant community grew even further when the commander-in-chief at Montreal, Jeffrey Amherst, urged the colonial governors of New Hampshire, Massachusetts and New York to send merchants to Quebec to provide "for the comfort of the troops and of a population that had been cut off from European sources of supplies for two years."[5]

By 1765 there were roughly one hundred male Protestants in Montreal, and half of these were merchants, although the size of their operations varied greatly. The information for the other two major cities is less reliable, but it is likely that the early English-speaking populations of Quebec and Trois-Rivières were equally involved in mercantile pursuits. Few other English speakers were to come to Quebec until the late 1770s. Finally aware that the New England farmers were not coming the British officials turned their attention to soldiers whom they hoped to make over into farmers. The Fraser Highlanders, for instance, were established along both shores of the St. Lawrence downstream from Quebec City in places such as Murray Bay (La Malbaie) and Fraserville (Rivière du Loup).

---

5. *Ibid.*, p. 104.

James McGill
(Public Archives of Canada, C-2873)

But these soldiers were not sufficiently numerous to tip the demographic balance of the colony, and as they married French-speaking women in the vicinity their successors became indistinguishable from other habitants. Accordingly, for nearly the first twenty years of British rule the English-speaking population was made up in large part of camp followers. As successive British governors were to discover to their dismay, these merchants were not the peaceable New England farmers they had hoped to rule.

Who were these first English-speaking Quebecers? Donald Creighton, who lionized these men in his *Empire of the St. Lawrence*, described them as a diverse lot, coming primarily from various parts of what was then the British empire. "There were a few foreigners, Wentzel, Ermatinger and Wadden, and the Jews, Solomons and Levy. John Askin and William Holmes were natives of Ireland. Allsopp, Oakes, Gregory, Lees, Molson, the Frobisher brothers and many others were English. From Scotland came George McBeath, Simon McTavish, Richard Dobie, the McGills, Finlays, Grants, Lymburners, and Mackenzies. A certain number of merchants were natives of the thirteen colonies and among these were Price, Heywood, [and] Alexander Henry."[6] What united these men, however, was a common desire to prosper by sending raw materials via the St. Lawrence to Britain, and in the 1760s this goal drew many of them mainly, but not exclusively, to the fur trade. George Allsopp, for instance, came to Quebec City in 1761 and by the end of the decade had interests in the Labrador fisheries and in the export of grain and timber, to go along with his involvement in the fur trade. That the opportunities available were everything that these merchants hoped for is evident in the fact that many of their families remained dominant forces in the Quebec

---

6. Creighton, p. 24.

economy well into the nineteenth century, and in a few cases up to the 1980s.

But in spite of the commercial success which these merchants achieved in Quebec, they gained a reputation as political troublemakers, what the first governor after the Proclamation of 1763, James Murray, called "the most cruel, ignorant, rapacious fanatics that ever existed." The single issue that brought out their venom was the reluctance of the governors of Quebec, first Murray and then his successor Guy Carleton, to enforce the various provisions of the Proclamation. From the governors' point of view the Proclamation could not be implemented because the hoped-for English majority had not emerged. How were the British officials supposed to deal with the French majority if its land system were discarded and its political views ignored? This question had particular importance in the 1760s and early 1770s as the American colonies to the south moved towards revolution. What the governors wanted to avoid was a situation in which the Canadiens might join up with the Americans, and to preclude this possibility they were prepared to make concessions to their new subjects even if it meant antagonizing the King's "old" subjects. Accordingly, in an ad hoc fashion French civil law was tolerated to allow the continued functioning of the seigneurial system. As for the promised elected assembly, it was never convened.

From the merchants' point of view, this was not an abstract political issue, but rather a question of business. They saw the seigneurial system, for instance, as an obstacle to profitmaking for a fee had to be paid to the seigneur following each land transfer. To men who had come to Quebec to make money, such an obstacle to speculative activities was unacceptable, and they let the governors know it. Ultimately, the merchants forced Murray's removal. They thought they had found their man when Carleton arrived, but they were also bitterly disappointed by him, particularly in his role in preparing the Quebec Act of 1774.

The Quebec Act was an indication of the political impotence of the English-speaking population as it then existed. With scarcely 1 % of the Quebec population, no matter how economically powerful the merchants might have been, the remaining 99 % had to be appeased as the American Revolution approached. In the second constitutional document tabled since the conquest, there was no reference to an elected assembly, while there was a commitment to the perpetuation of French civil law. The only significant change from the situation that had existed between 1763 and 1774 was the expansion of the territory of Quebec. In 1763 it was defined as a small rectangular area in the St. Lawrence Valley, but now it was to include much of present day Ontario as well as parts of what would soon belong to the United States.

Angered by the lack of concessions in their direction in the Quebec Act, a few merchants flirted with the idea of joining the Americans in the revolution as an act of protest. Ultimately, most came to recognize that their economic interests were too closely tied to Britain to risk independence. But while they rejected the revolution, some of the merchants hoped that they might profit from it by reason of its unsettling effect upon American colonists who wished to continue living under British rule. If these Loyalists were to come to Quebec in sufficiently large numbers, then the English-speaking majority that had been hoped for in 1763 might still be created; and if an English-speaking majority were created how could British authorities then continue to ignore the need for British laws and institutions?

2. The Loyalists

The term "Loyalist" is a much misused term in Canadian history. Technically, it should refer solely to those people who came to the British North American colonies during or immediately after the American Revolution so as to continue to live under British rule. But while the war ended in 1783, it is not very difficult to find people who crossed the new border as late as 1800 referring to themselves as "late Loyalists".

That they were late in comparison with those who arrived in the early 1780s there can be no doubt, but whether they had been loyal to the Crown was another question, particularly as some of them had fought on the American side in the revolution. These Americans will be discussed in the following section of this chapter, while this section will deal with the true Loyalists. Relatively few of the real Loyalists came to settle in the territory now known as Quebec, but such might not have been the case if the merchants of Montreal and Quebec City had had their way. Once again, however, these men saw their interests sacrificed in the name of British colonial policy. From the start of the Loyalist migrations to the Province of Quebec, British policy sought to isolate these newcomers both from the boundaries with their former homeland and from the French majority. Keeping Loyalists away from the American border was seen as a means of reducing the possibility of renewed conflict. Accordingly, there was a prohibition against settlement in the area that would later become the Eastern Townships. Instead, there was to be a "cordon sanitaire" between the New England states and the seigneurial settlements along the St. Lawrence Valley. In spite of orders to the contrary, some squatters erected houses in the vicinity of Missisquoi Bay, but these were later destroyed upon the command of Governor Haldimand. There can be little doubt, however, that had the colonial office been willing to encourage Loyalist settlement in the region that large numbers of people could have been attracted. The Eastern Townships region formed a geographical extension of northern New England, and when the prohibition was lifted in 1792 the Americans came in large numbers.

The settlement of Loyalists in what is now known as Quebec was also impeded by the British desire to segregate them from the existing French population. The fear was that the Loyalists might antagonize the habitants whose favour was still being courted by the British. With the Eastern Townships out of the question, the lands to the north of Lake Ontario thus became the area to which most Loyalists were sent within the old Province of Quebec. The St. Lawrence Valley served largely as a reception area for people who were in passage, most often on their way west. For instance, Machiche (Yamachiche), along the north shore of Lac St-Pierre between Montreal and Trois-Rivières, served as a temporary home for Loyalists between 1778 and 1784. There were roughtly 160 émigrés there in 1778, a number that peaked at 325 in 1781 before gradually falling off.[7] Most of those who departed from Machiche headed for the Lake Ontario region, as was also the case for those who passed through Sorel. The seigneury there was purchased by the Crown to accommodate Loyalists, and the name of the town was anglicized so that it was known as Wiliam Henry, in honour of a future King of England, until 1845. In fact, few Loyalists actually settled in Sorel. In 1783 alone roughly 1,400 were sent there, but departures reduced the number to only 300 by early 1784.

---

7. Esther Barnett, "Loyalist Settlement on the Gaspé Peninsula", M.A. Thesis, Bishop's University, 1973.

The British hardly encouraged the Loyalists to remain in the area to the east of the Ottawa River. Most of this area was declared off-limits for various reasons, but the Gaspé peninsula satisfied the requirement of being neither near the American border nor close to any significant concentration of French speakers. As the British were trying to empty the temporary camps of their residents in 1783 and 1784, the Gaspé became the destination of approximately 500 people divided initially betwen Douglastown on the coast of the Gulf of St. Lawrence and New Carlisle on the shores of the Baie des Chaleurs. Given the choice between the Gaspé and the lands of what would soon be Upper Canada, it is little wonder that most of the Loyalists headed west.

By 1785 the 500 Loyalists in the Gaspé made up half of the total Loyalist population in the Province of Quebec east of the Ottawa River, while the other half was scattered among various towns. The bulk of the Loyalists, nearly 6,000, lived to the west of the Ottawa, a distribution that took on great significance in the history of English-speaking Quebec when in 1791 the old Province of Quebec was divided into Upper Canada (Ontario) and Lower Canada (Quebec). This division removed the majority of the Loyalists of central Canada from Quebec history, and left English-speaking Quebec with less than 10,000 people after thirty years of British rule, or British neglect as the merchants might have put it. Natural increase had played a major role in reaching the 10,000 figure, together with whatever chance migration took place. The British made no effort to encourage immigration while the seigneurial system remained in force. However, in 1791, the same year that the Province of Quebec was split in two, significant steps were taken to remove that major obstacle to the growth of the English-speaking population.

3. The Americans

The Constitutional Act of 1791 was the third attempt on the part of the British in as many decades to find a satisfactory political structure for the territories in the St. Lawrence Valley. In the short term, this act had a devastating effect upon English-speaking Quebec because the English speakers within the old Province of Quebec were divided, almost evenly, between two jurisdictions. London was interested in encouraging the settlement of Upper Canada which was clearly going to develop as an overwhelmingly British colony. Prior to 1791, however, the rules of the seigneurial system technically extended to the western lands. By establishing the separate colony of Upper Canada, British law was to have free rein.

For the English speakers in Lower Canada, however, British law still did not govern all aspects of their lives. Nevertheless, the Constitutional Act did provide at least some satisfaction for the demands of the leading merchants by ordering that land which had not yet been surveyed could in the future be held according to free and common soccage. The seigneurial system was to be restricted to those areas where it already existed, particularly in the St. Lawrence Valley, but land might be owned outright in all other parts of Lower Canada. In the immediate aftermath of the Conquest, the British authorities had proposed such a landholding system for all of Quebec, but in the face of little demand for these lands they backed down so as not to alienate the French. Now they were prepared to try to use land policy once again to attract New Englanders. This time they tried to avoid alienating the French by leaving existing seigneurial lands untouched, and the policy worked.

Between 1791 and the War of 1812 Americans pushed across the border in large numbers in search of

Philemon Wright
(Public Archives of Canada, C-123938)

Kilborn's Mills, a settlement in the Eastern Townships at the American border (Public Archives of Canada, C-9460)

lands that they could now hold upon terms with which they were familiar. One estimate sets the number of these English speakers in the Eastern Townships at 15,000 by 1807.[8] Americans also moved into the Ottawa Valley, where they were particularly conspicuous in the establishment of such settlements as Hull. Between 1791 and 1812 the English-speaking population of Lower Canada increased from 10,000 to 30,000 and nearly all of this increase can be attributed to the arrival of the Americans.

When the British established their policy for the previously unsurveyed lands, they did more than establish new rules for landholding. At the same time, they also put into place the leader and associate system to persuade Americans to come north. The areas in question were divided into townships which in turn were divided into lots. All or part of each township was then granted to a team headed by a leader who was joined by a number of associates. By July 1793 petitions for land had already been received from 256 leaders who represented 10,000 associates, and by 1809 10 million acres had been promised to various teams.[9] This system had the virtue of having been employed at an earlier date in the settlement of parts of New England. It was therefore hoped that New Englanders would be encouraged to take part in the push north if the system employed were familiar to them. The problem with the leader and associate system, however, was that it was open to abuse by speculators who posed as leaders but who had no real associates to join them. It was estimated that 2 million acres of Eastern Townships land were in the hands of speculators by

8. M.L. Hansen and J.B. Brebner, *The Mingling of the Canadian and American Peoples* (New York, 1970), p. 74.

9. *Ibid.*; G.F. McGuigan, "Une Analyse Historique: Land Policy and Land Disposal Under Tenure of Free and Common Soccage in Quebec and Lower Canada, 1763-1809", Ph.D. Thesis, Université Laval, 1962.

1809. [10] Among the leading speculators were camp followers such as Hugh Finlay, who by the 1790s had achieved considerable influence in the new government of Lower Canada. There was a certain irony in the fact that the merchants, who had long complained about the policies of the colonial governors, were now proving an obstacle to English-speaking settlement in Lower Canada.

In fairness to the leader and associate system, it did contribute to the settlement of 2 million acres of land in the Eastern Townships and the Ottawa Valley prior to the start of the War of 1812. [11] The system succeeded, for instance, in bringing Philemon Wright and a group of settlers from Massachusetts to settle at Hull in 1800. In this and in other cases, the system placed English speakers on the land, but at the same time it created a sort of local aristocracy as the leader retained large quantities of land for himself. In the case of Hull, the Wrights grafted a thriving lumber business onto their agricultural pursuits to turn Hull into a veritable company town. Settlers also chafed under rules that set aside one-seventh of all land in each township as Crown reserves with a similar amount of land being reserved for the support of the Protestant clergy. In 1795 it was decided to scatter these reserves throughout each township, but since these lands were set aside as a speculative source of income for the government of Lower Canada and the Protestant clergy they stood as an obstacle to farmers who might have wanted to expand their holdings.

The historian G.F. McGuigan has argued that these various problems prevented the migration of Americans from being larger than it was, and this may well have been the case. [12] Nevertheless, these Ameri-

---

10. McGuigan, "Une Analyse Historique".
11. *Ibid.*
12. *Ibid.*

cans helped triple the English-speaking population between 1791 and 1812. In the process, the English-speaking population reached 10 % of the total population of Lower Canada. More significantly, however, the Americans transformed this population from one which had been largely urban and led by a small British merchant elite, many of whom were Anglicans, into a much more diverse group. The camp followers were now joined by Americans whose political values were frequently different from their own, whose economic position as farmers was certainly different, and whose religion often differed for many of the newcomers were Methodists. Moreover, to the extent that the Americans came to identify with the regions in which they settled, they developed political demands that frequently differed from those of the urban merchants. But while the Americans brought a certain diversity to the English-speaking population, their impact was minor compared to that of the English speakers who were to arrive over the next 35 years.

4. Britain's Dispossessed

During the first half century of British rule in Quebec there were relatively few immigrants who actually made the journey across the Atlantic. To be sure, a boatload of Scots arrived in Quebec in 1786, and there were Irish immigrants who could be found prior to 1815 in the Gaspé, the Ottawa Valley, and the colony's two major towns. However, these sporadic migrations did not form part of any substantial movement in the way that the Americans crossed the border in waves between 1791 and 1812. The American pipeline from New England was shut off first by war and later by the increasingly easy access to western lands in the United States. However, at roughly the same time that one source of recruits for the English-speaking population was drying up, a new source was emerging in Britain with the end of the Napoleonic wars in 1815, which provided the opportunity for the dispossessed of England, Scotland and Ireland to seek relief in British North America. Now that the seas were relatively safe, shipowners were pleased to convey emigrants as a west-bound cargo to take the place of the timber they had carried to Britain. As for the British government, it now had large numbers of de-mobilized soldiers on its hands and was increasingly willing to assist in the disposal of its surplus population.

Some of those who came to British North America were relatively well-to-do. Within the Irish population, for instance, there were those in Quebec City with sufficient means to fight for the establishment of their own Catholic church in the 1820s.[13] There were also Irish Protestants such as Thomas Workman who achieved a position of importance in the Montreal business community. Such individuals were the exception, however, as the bulk of the British emigrants had been dispossessed either because of the Industrial Revolution, which made certain trades unnecessary, or through crises in rural areas caused by crop failures and by the efforts to drive out small landholders to create large farms. In Scotland both the urban and the rural crises were evident. In the cities weavers were put out of work by the growth of industrial production, while in the Highlands the crofters were chased from their lands as landlords discovered that "large sheep and cattle farms as well as deer parks were more profitable than poor tenants."[14]

Starting from a mere trickle in 1815 the number of emigrants leaving British ports for British North America reached 23,000 in 1819, 66,000 in 1832, and a

---

13. Marianna O'Gallagher, *Saint Patrick's, Quebec* (Quebec, 1981).
14. Lynda Price, *Introduction to the Social History of Scots in Quebec* (Ottawa, 1981), p. 3.

high of 109,600 during the Irish potato famine of 1847. A large number of those who left Britain never reached the British North American ports having succumbed to illness and disease in passage. In 1847, for instance, 16 % of all those who left for North America died on the way over. As for those who made it to the other side of the Atlantic, many probably never set foot in Quebec since they landed at one of the Maritime ports without the slightest intention of going to Quebec. Such was the case for over 20 % of those who left for British North America in 1832. Moreover, many who disembarked at Quebec City were merely on their way to other destinations in North America. While nearly 750,000 immigrants landed at Quebec City between 1829 and 1853, the English-speaking population increased by only 140,000 and some of this was due to natural increase. It was estimated that in 1826 only 5 % of the immigrants arriving in Quebec City remained in the colony, and historian Helen Cowan has gone so far as to say that the immigrants had little impact upon Quebec.[15]

While the significance of the British migrations might have been greater had a larger number remained in Quebec, there can be little doubt as to the influence of those who did stay. It is useful, for instance, to note that by the time of Confederation the Irish made up the most important ethnic group among English-speaking Quebecers, followed by the English and then the Scots. This ranking was merely a reflection of the distribution of the immigrants who landed at Quebec City between 1824 and 1853. Of these immigrants, 60 % were Irish, 29 % English and 11 % Scottish, and a sufficient number remained to push the English-speaking population to 25 % of the Quebec total by the start of the 1850s. This increased English-

---

15. Helen Cowan, *British Emigration to British North America* (Toronto, 1961), p. 185.

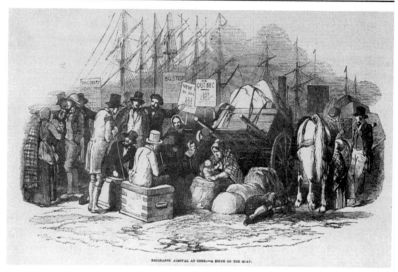

Irish emigrants on the quay at Cork
(Public Archives of Canada, C-3904)

The quarantine station on Grosse Isle, 1850
(Public Archives of Canada, C-12085)

speaking presence was even more pronounced in those parts of the colony where enclaves of English speakers already existed before 1815. In both Montreal and Quebec City these immigrants made their presence felt initially through the diseases that many brought with them. In the 1830s a quarantine station was established at Grosse Isle, thirty miles downstream from Quebec City, to try to keep disease away from the two major cities. This precaution was to no avail, however, as cholera took its toll in 1832, followed by typhus in 1847. These diseases eventually passed, but many of the immigrants remained, raising the English-speaking population of Quebec City to 40 % by 1851. In several sectors of the city English-speaking majorities existed. In Montreal the impact was even more profound as an absolute majority of the city's population was English-speaking as early as the 1830s. This situation would only change following the arrival of large numbers of French speakers from rural Quebec in the 1850s and 1860s.

In both cities English speakers tended to inhabit the western sections, a pattern that still existed at the start of the 1980s. But while the English segregated themselves residentially from the French population, many of the new English speakers shared the jobs at the lower end of the economic ladder with their French-speaking counterparts. This, too, was a major change from the pre-1815 period when English speakers were heavily concentrated in the leading positions in the economy.

British immigrants were conspicuous in Quebec's two major cities, but most of them actually settled in various rural parts of the colony. In 1851 only one-third of all British-born residents were living in Quebec's major centres. By that date English speakers made up a majority of the residents of the Ottawa Valley because of the impact of the post-1815 migrations. Scots and Irish Protestants settled in the region downstream from Hull, while Irish Catholics were dominant upstream, having been drawn to the region by the jobs available building the Rideau Canal and having stayed because of the employment offered by the timber trade. The presence of these Irish Catholics prompted geographer Raoul Blanchard to describe the region as "Petite Irlande". [16]

Immigrants from Britain were also attracted to areas closer to the American border where English speakers from the south had settled prior to the War of 1812. In the southwest corner of the colony, in the Huntingdon area, many of the American settlers had returned to the United States with the outbreak of war. Their places were taken by Protestant immigrants from Britain. Robert Sellar, the editor of the *Huntingdon Gleaner*, could later claim that when he arrived in Huntingdon County in 1863 it was "as solidly Protestant as any [county] in Ontario." [17] To the east, in the area normally known as the Eastern Townships, the Americans did not depart during the War of 1812, and British immigrants came to join them in the decades that followed. For instance, there were the farmers who settled in Megantic County in 1828 after their expulsion from the Island of Arran in Scotland.

It was hoped by some that further British settlement in the region might be encouraged by the establishment of the British American Land Company in 1834. The company acquired 850,000 acres of land, roughly two-thirds of which consisted of unsurveyed territory in the eastern section of the region. The firm was headed by various prominent Montreal merchants, including Peter McGill whose adopted family had amassed considerable wealth since the Conquest. The merchants hoped to gain further profits through

16. Raoul Blanchard, *L'Ouest du Canada-français* (Montreal, 1953), II, p. 77.
17. Robert Sellar, *The Tragedy of Quebec* (Toronto, 1974), p. 8.

their land dealings, but at the same time they claimed an interest in building up the English-speaking population at a moment when the political movement of Louis-Joseph Papineau was edging ever closer to rebellion. In line with the actions of the English-speaking merchant elite since the Conquest, the merchants of the 1830s could see the political advantage of building up the ranks of the English-speaking population to bolster their own status. However, as had been the case earlier in the century with the introduction of the leader and associate system, the lure of speculative dollars was greater than the merchants' interest in throwing their lands open to British immigrants. Some effort was made to bring out Highland Scots in the 1830s, but by and large the land company was more interested in buying additional land than it was in selling what it already held. This costly policy forced it to relinquish much of its land to the Crown in the early 1840s, and it only began to seek out settlers for its remaining lands in the late 1840s. By then, however, many immigrants who might have been drawn to the Eastern Townships had gone elsewhere.

5. Conclusion

It is tempting to think of the growth of the English-speaking population from the Conquest to Confederation in terms of what might have been. What percentage of the Quebec population would have been English-speaking had the British devised a different policy towards the Loyalists, had the leader and associate system been formulated more wisely, or had means been taken to try to keep more of the post-1815 immigrants from Britain in Quebec? Such questions had a certain relevance by the 1850s when the flow of British emigrants to the port of Quebec slowed considerably. In 1859, for instance, 8,778 Britons disembarked at Quebec, only 10 % of the number for the peak year of 1847. In fact, during the quarter century beginning in 1855 there were only as many arrivals as there had been in the previous decade. With the close of substantial British immigration English-speaking Quebec was left, for the first time since 1791, with no ready source of new recruits, a situation that coincided in the 1860s with the first significant exodus of those already settled in Quebec from both Quebec City and the Eastern Townships. The percentage of the Quebec population that was English-speaking ceased to increase after 1851, and in the 1860s an absolute decline was recorded.

The comings and goings of these various groups of immigrants influenced the overall size of the English-speaking population. At the same time the movement of these groups created an increasingly diverse population in the century leading up to Confederation. In the early years following the Conquest there was a certain common identity among English speakers as the camp followers dominated the scene, but this situation changed as immigration picked up. By the time of Confederation, there were still English speakers interested in international trade, but the majority were concerned with farming, fishing, or the mere task of survival. Some thought of themselves as Americans, others as Irishmen, and still others as Scots; some were Catholics while others belonged to a variety of Protestant denominations; most identified with that part of Quebec where they lived. Having established themselves in Quebec, these English speakers dealt with each other and with the French majority on the basis of these various identities. The precise nature of this interaction will be the focus of the remaining chapters of Part I.

SELECT BIBLIOGRAPHY

Burt, A.L. *The Old Province of Quebec.* Toronto, 1933.

Cowan, Helen. *British Emigration to North America.* Toronto, 1961.

Creighton, Donald. *Empire of the St. Lawrence.* Toronto, 1956.

Hansen, M.L. and J.B. Brebner, *The Mingling of the Canadian and American Peoples.* New York, 1970.

Ouellet, Fernand. *Economic and Social History of Quebec, 1760-1850.* Ottawa, 1980.

III

The Economic Structure
of English-Speaking Quebec

Numerous observers of Quebec affairs have commented upon the symbolism of the two nineteenth century buildings that dominate Place d'Armes in Montreal. To the north of the square is the headquarters of the Bank of Montreal, built in 1848, which to many links English speakers with the management of the economy. To the south is Notre-Dame Basilica, also constructed in the pre-Confederation period, and symbolic of the concern of the French majority for the preservation of its culture. By viewing this concern for cultural survival as inconsistent with an active role in the economy, some observers of the architecture of Place d'Armes have concluded that all English speakers were involved in running the economy while the French were their employees. This neat division of Quebec into the English rulers and the French ruled has been given a lasting place in many people's minds by Hugh MacLennan's novel *Two Solitudes*.[1] In the literature more familiar to specialists in Quebec history, this same conception is central to such works as Donald Creighton's *Empire of the St. Lawrence*. On the

1. Hugh MacLennan, *Two Solitudes* (Toronto, 1945).

one hand, there were the English speakers participating in a trans-Atlantic economy; on the other there were the French who were "sullen, suspicious and unresponsive" when it came to economic issues.[2]

Like all caricatures, this neat division of the Quebec population has survived remarkably well over time because it does possess an element of truth. Clearly, the most important figures who ran the pre-Confederation Quebec economy were English speakers; rare were the French speakers who operated any businesses of significant dimensions. However, the linguistic division of the economy breaks down once one moves below the highest positions. At the lower strata, it becomes more difficult to identify occupations that were exclusively dominated by the English from those which were the preserves of the French. As Table 3.1 indicates, the overall occupational structure of the British origin population in 1871 was not all that different from the structure of the French population. In fact, there were more significant differences within the English-speaking population than there were between the English and the French. Take, for instance, the occupation of labourer where the French-English gap was relatively small compared to that between Irish Catholics and Scots.

As the Table 3.1 indicates, the English-speaking population occupied a variety of roles within the pre-Confederation economy. This chapter describes that diversity of economic experience.

---

2. Creighton, p. 154; a similar characterization of the French is provided in Everett Hughes' *French Canada in Transition* (Chicago, 1963).

TABLE 3.1

Occupations and Ethnic Origins:
Quebec, 1871

	ETHNIC ORIGIN						
Occupation	Que-becers	French	All British	Irish Cath.	Irish Prot.	Eng-lish	Scots
Farmers	54.6	56.1	52.8	41.1	59.8	43.2	60.1
Manufacturers /Merchants	6.2	5.4	7.1	9.3	5.7	10.6	7.6
Professionals	3.2	2.5	4.0	3.5	3.7	9.4	5.2
White Collar	3.2	2.5	4.0	5.2	4.6	8.2	3.8
Artisans	13.2	12.4	14.7	17.2	14.1	17.0	14.5
Semi-skilled	4.9	4.9	4.9	6.8	3.8	4.0	3.4
Labourers	13.0	14.4	11.4	15.4	6.1	6.5	3.2
Servants	1.7	1.8	1.6	1.5	2.2	1.1	2.2
	100 %	100 %	100 %	100 %	100 %	100 %	100 %

Source: A. Gordon Darroch and Michael Ornstein, "Ethnicity and Oc-cupational Structure in Canada in 1871", *Canadian Historical Review*, LXI (1980), 326-7.

1. The Business Elite

Few would argue that English speakers held the bulk of power in the pre-Confederation economy of Quebec. The largest commercial houses, the most important banks and the major factories were all under the control of English speakers, most of whom lived in Montreal or Quebec City. But even when one looks at the lesser business activities across the colony the English had a presence that was all out of proportion to their place in the population. For instance, in 1842 English speakers made up one-third of the busi-nessmen in the rural parishes of St-Eustache, St-Benoît, and Ste-Scholastique even though only 4 % of the local population was English-speaking.[3]

3. Ouellet, *Lower Canada*, p. 163.

It is easy, and therefore tempting, to ascribe the success of this small cluster of English speakers to their way of thinking about business matters that differed markedly from that of the French majority. Historian Fernand Ouellet has written much about the *mentalité* of the French-speakers, noting that their Catholic up-bringing stood in the way of their aggressively seizing business opportunities.[4] Since the Irish Catholics rarely shared in the running of the Quebec economy, there is even further circumstantial support for this *mentalité* interpretation. What such a view ignores, however, are the specific economic circumstances that permitted a small group of English-speaking Protestants to seize control of the Quebec economy in the aftermath of the Conquest. Once this control had been achieved, it only grew in years to follow.

Historian José Igartua has convincingly demon-strated that the quick rise to prominence of English-speaking merchants in the years immediately after the Conquest was due to "a change in climate".[5] French-speaking merchants who had been involved in a variety of economic endeavours, the most important of which was the fur trade, were quickly pushed from the scene by the radical redefinition of the economy after 1759. These French merchants found that military and government contracts from which they had gained a considerable portion of their livelihood were now lost to the camp followers, and that their access to the markets and credit facilities of France was now useless as London had taken on primary importance. Some partnerships existed between French and English mer-chants in the early years of British rule with the former feeding their knowledge of local circumstances to the latter. Naturally, however, this information became

---

4. Ouellet, *Economic and Social History*, p. 608.
5. José Igartua, "A Change in Climate: The Conquest and the Mar-chands of Montreal", Canadian Historical Association *Historical Papers* (hereafter *CHA Papers*), 1974.

less and less essential over time, and the French were slowly squeezed out of the fur trade by English speakers, most notably by the establishment of the North West Company in 1779.

Most of the members of this company, which came to occupy a central place in the major economic activity of the immediate post-Conquest era, were Scots, and throughout much of the pre-Confederation period members of this segment of the English-speaking population were conspicuous in the boardrooms of Montreal and Quebec City. This success was not due, however, to religion or any other aspect of one's upbringing. Rather, the achievements of the Scottish businessmen were linked to concrete developments within the eighteenth century economy of Scotland. As David Macmillan has observed, "The society of central Scotland was one that had 'taken off' by 1770 into a phase of rapid industrial growth... [which] was matched by an even more remarkable increase in foreign trade."[6] Scottish businessmen who were looking for an ever-widening field for their economic ambitions actively lobbied for the retention of Quebec in the early 1760s when it appeared that Britain might give back to France at the conference table what it had won on the battlefield. In 1763 Quebec came firmly under British rule, and the Scots moved in to reap the benefits.

These Scots did not content themselves for long with running the fur trade. Soon, they and other English-speaking merchants in the colony began to diversify their activities. There was the case, for instance, of the Scot, James Dunlop, who arrived in Montreal in 1776 by way of the American colonies to the south. With connections in the major Scottish port

6. David Macmillan. "The New Men in Action: Scottish Mercantile and Shipping Operations in the North American Colonies, 1760-1825", in Macmillan, ed., *Canadian Business History: Selected Studies* (Toronto, 1971), p. 45.

John Molson
(Public Archives of Canada,
C-5968)

Bank of Montreal Head Office
(Public Archives of Canada,
C-20533)

of Greenock, Dunlop involved himself at first in the import of textiles, liquors and groceries, before also becoming interested in the export of wheat and timber. This multiplicity of interests also marked the careers of other early English-speaking businessmen. In Quebec City George Allsopp combined the fur trade with an interest in the Labrador fisheries, while John Molson was involved in both the fur and grain trades. This diversification was absolutely crucial to the continued power of these men into the early nineteenth century when the fur trade fell into decline. As the export of grain and timber came to replace that of furs, English-speaking businessmen were in an ideal position to add to their wealth and power. A typical member of the new generation of businessmen who had not been involved with the fur trade was George Moffat, who established himself in Montreal at the start of the 1800s before going on to occupy a central role in the movement of grain from Upper Canada to Liverpool via Montreal. As for the timber trade Philemon Wright of Hull and William Price of Quebec City were also looking to new export markets as the 1800s began.

These men involved in the movement of the new staples sought to further their interests by improving the transportation facilities in the colony. The numerous rapids in the Great Lakes - St. Lawrence system could be tolerated in the fur trade for a high price could be secured for a commodity that was not particularly bulky and which could easily be transported around the rapids. By contrast, it was essential to ship thousands of pounds of the new staples to turn a profit, and this led to the need first for canals and later for railroads. In both of these pursuits, not surprisingly, the English-speaking business elite played a central role. From the 1810s through to the 1840s the government provided the funds for canal construction, but members of the elite frequently provided the direction.

John Richardson, one of the mainstays of the Montreal business community, headed the commission formed to build the Lachine Canal. As for the railways, private firms built and controlled the various lines that were constructed beginning in the late 1830s, although government support was always present. Invariably, the boards of directors of these lines included members of the business elite. Accordingly, when the building of the St. Lawrence and Atlantic Railway was proposed in the 1840s to connect Montreal with Portland, Maine, the Molsons and the McGills had their places on the board of directors.

These same people were also active in lobbying the Lower Canadian government to authorize the establishment of the first chartered banks. The grain trade demanded that merchants have sufficient funds on hand at harvest time to pay the farmers for their crops. Rare was the merchant who had such funds at his disposal, and this is where the banks entered the scene. The merchants wanted the government to authorize the establishment of institutions which could issue paper money that might then be paid to farmers. The idea was that the merchants would pool their resources to provide the capital for the banks, which could then issue notes up to the value of their capital. The merchants could then borrow these notes to pay the farmers, and it was expected that the farmers would accept the notes because of the government's backing of the project. The rules of the game were fixed so that if the banks failed the holder of the notes would be left with worthless paper, while the operators of the bank, that is the merchants, would get off relatively cheaply. Given terms that so favoured the merchant elite, it is not surprising that such men dominated Quebec's first two banks, the Bank of Montreal, chartered in 1818, and the Quebec Bank which opened in the following year.

By the middle of the nineteenth century, the English-speaking business leaders of Quebec City and Montreal were involved in a variety of economic activities closely connected with the export of timber and grain. As long as these staple trades were healthy, these English speakers stood to increase their power and influence. However, in the decade leading up to Confederation the timber trade of Quebec City fell on hard times, thus provoking a movement from the town of some of its major businessmen as well as many English speakers who laboured for them. By the 1850s the foreign market for squared timber was drying up, with its place being taken by sawn lumber. This new product could be shipped from Montreal, thanks to the deepening of the channel between Quebec's two major centres and the emergence of the steamship as a vehicle which could easily navigate these waters. Slowly but surely, the Quebec City coves where timber had previously been stored became stagnant, and the shipyards where numerous vessels had been constructed laid off many of their workers, whose numbers had reached 4,600 by 1847. Henceforth, there was little incentive for the most aggressive of the English-speaking businessmen to go to Quebec City, but some incentive for those who were there to leave or at least to invest elsewhere. As will be shown in more detail later, the English-speaking employees connected with this declining trade simply moved on to other parts of the continent.

Thus, the focus of business activity centered in Montreal by the mid-1800s. In the corridors of the Board of Trade one could find men involved in the staple trades, transportation ventures, and banking. By mid-century, one could also increasingly find men involved with manufacturing. In one way or another, many of the new factories were linked to the staple trades and to the facilities they required. This was particularly true for the Ogilvie flour mill and the

Timber coves and sailing ships at Quebec City
(Public Archives of Canada, C-6073)

An early view of Sherbrooke
(Public Archives of Canada, C-23387)

Molson brewery. There were also large facilities to build engines for steamboats, such as the Eagle Foundry operated by John Ward. Later in the century, with the arrival of the railway age, one of the most important employers was the Grand Trunk Railway whose shops at Pointe St-Charles in Montreal gave work to nearly 800 men in 1871.[7] The connection with transportation could be seen in other ways as well; the Lachine Canal provided a source of power for industrial production, while the railway provided the means to connect factories with a larger market. The new factories that were emerging by the mid-1800s were almost invariably under the control of English speakers. Sometimes they were artisans who had accumulated sufficient capital to set themselves up as factory owners, while in other cases they were merchants who could see the potential profits from producing goods in addition to selling them. Such was the experience, for instance, of the importers Brown and Childs who had moved into manufacturing and were employing 800 workers in their shoe factory by 1856.

By the time of Confederation there were English-speaking businessmen of note to be found in Quebec outside of the limits of Montreal. In addition to those linked to the timber trade of the Ottawa Valley and Quebec City, there was an increasingly important group of businessmen in the Eastern Townships, concentrated in Sherbrooke. The maturing of this local elite was symbolized by the establishment of the Eastern Townships Bank that opened for business in 1859. Influential in the bank's affairs were two men with connections with the British American Land Company. Alexander Galt was commissioner from 1844 to 1855, and was followed by R.W. Heneker from 1855 to 1902.

---

7. Paul Craven and Tom Traves, "Canadian Railways as Manufacturers, 1850-1880", *CHA Papers*, 1983, pp. 254-281.

Both of these men were active in the promotion of railway construction across the region, and in 1866 Heneker played a leading role in the establishment of what was to become Sherbrooke's most important employer, the Paton Manufacturing Company.

Sherbrooke's English-speaking business elite, like that of Montreal, had its hands in a variety of economic activities. The Sherbrooke elite could not have existed, however, without the support of the English business community of Montreal. For instance, Galt secured the routing of the St. Lawrence and Atlantic Railway through Sherbrooke because of his ties to Montreal interests, while Heneker's close links with major Montreal figures such as George Stephen assured the construction of the Paton woollen mill. These connections were encouraged by the fact that both Galt and Heneker were English-speaking and had been born in Britain. They had an affinity with the leading lights in Montreal that French-speaking leaders could not possess.[8] The presence of a powerful English-speaking elite in Montreal also had its impact on the existence of less influential English-speaking businessmen elsewhere in Quebec.

By Confederation, however, the influence of the Montreal elite went well beyond the boundaries of the province. The railroads controlled by these men extended from the Atlantic as far west as Sarnia, and their banks had branches across a similarly large area. Their factories sent goods to distant markets, while the ships they controlled made regular trips to Britain. On the basis of this economic power, members of the Montreal élite were in a position to influence all aspects of political and economic life. Their political prowess was evident in their ability to shape the

---

8. Ronald Rudin, *Banking en français* (Toronto, 1985).

British North America Act, an issue that will be discussed in Chapter V. Their economic power gave them the ability to mold the lives of the English speakers who worked for them.

2. The Urban Labourers

The beginnings of large-scale industrialization at Montreal together with the problems faced by farmers in various parts of the province led to a greater concentration of Quebecers within the city of Montreal in the years leading up to Confederation. While 6 % of all Quebecers lived in the city in 1851, the figure reached 9 % twenty years later. The 1871 census recorded the Montreal population as having exceeded 100,000 for the first time, and it also reported a French majority in the city for the first time since the 1830s. Simultaneously, however, English speakers were also entering the city in large numbers so that between 1851 and 1871 the percentage of Quebec's English speakers living in Montreal grew from 14 % to 18 %. Of the nearly 50,000 English speakers inhabiting the city in 1871, only a small fraction were the directors of the economy discussed in the previous section, while large numbers laboured as their employees. Nor was the presence of English speakers among the labouring classes a new development only evident towards the end of the pre-Confederation period. In Quebec City, where the English-speaking population only fell off in the decade leading up to 1867, English speakers were disproportionately represented as early as 1831 not only within the ranks of businessmen and professionals, but also among artisans and day labourers. As Table 3.2 indicates, a similar situation existed in Montreal.

TABLE 3.2

English Speakers in the Occupational Structure
of Montreal and Quebec City, 1831

% of English-Speakers in Each Category

	QUEBEC CITY	MONTREAL
Total population	33 %	50 %
Businessmen	55	65
Professionals	54	60
Artisans	39	55
Day Labourers	51	53

Source: Fernand Ouellet, "Structures des occupations et ethnicité dans les villes de Québec et Montréal", in *Éléments d'histoire sociale du Bas-Canada* (Montreal, 1972), pp. 177-202.

In both Quebec City and Montreal there was a considerable difference between the lives of skilled English-speaking workers and those who served as menial labourers. In the former category were men who were often brought from Britain to Quebec by the English-speaking business elite. In Quebec City this included the various skilled craftsmen who were brought in to work in the shipbuilding trade. Other tradesmen, such as brewers and hatters also could be found in the employ of men of their own nationality. Historian D.T. Ruddell has noted: "English and Scottish merchants and craftsmen practiced national exclusivity [in Quebec City as they] recruited partners and employees from their home regions."[9] Nor was the situation very different in Montreal, particularly in the iron and steel trades for which the best craftsmen in the world could be found in Britain. Some of these men worked on their own in small shops, while others were employed in larger facilities such as the massive repair shops of the Grand Trunk Railway.

9. D.T. Ruddel, "Quebec City, 1765-1831: The Evolution of a Colonial Town", Ph.D. Thesis, Université Laval, 1981, p. 354.

Many of the British craftsmen who arrived in Quebec found their lives undergoing rapid change as early as the second quarter of the nineteenth century. Their skills were jeopardized by the rise of industrial production that threatened to replace their crafts by the use of new machinery and masses of unskilled labourers. Ruddell has described the first strike in Quebec City as having been waged by English-speaking hatters in the 1820s who were concerned about their lot.[10] Similarly, Joanne Burgess has shown that apprentice shoemakers in both Montreal and Quebec City were concerned as early as the 1830s by a situation in which they were being reduced from the status of skilled craftsmen-in-training to that of wage labourers.[11]

By the third quarter of the century the ranks of the English speakers among the unskilled labourers were swollen because of the growth of factory production and the arrival of the Irish in large numbers. H.C. Pentland has asserted that "until about 1860 the Irish made the unskilled urban employment of Lower Canada pretty much their own preserve."[12] One could legitimately have gained such an impression from walking through the working class area of Griffintown that bordered on the Lachine Canal. In the years leading up to Confederation, the Irish could be found in the shoe factory of Brown and Childs and in the DeWitt Buckskin Glove Factory. In both firms, the process of mechanization had made it possible for all members of the family to serve as labourers.[13] Elsewhere in

---

10. *Ibid.*
11. Joanne Burgess, "L'industrie de la chaussure à Montréal, 1840-1870: le passage de l'artisanat à la fabrique", *Revue d'histoire de l'Amérique française*, XXXI (1977), pp. 187-210.
12. H.C. Pentland, *Labour and Capital in Canada* (Toronto, 1981), p. 119.
13. Bettina Bradbury, "The Family Economy and Work in an Industrializing City", *CHA Papers*, 1979, p. 75.

Montreal, Irishmen were engaged as labourers in the two major construction projects of the pre-Confederation period, the building of the Lachine Canal and of the Victoria Bridge. They similarly provided their brawn for projects such as the digging of the Rideau Canal and the laying of tracks for the St. Lawrence and Atlantic Railway in the Eastern Townships. [14]

In Quebec City Irish labourers were particularly conspicuous in the more menial jobs connected with the timber trade and the shipbuilding industry before both fell on hard times in the 1850s. Largely excluded from the jobs requiring skills, the Irish found themselves concentrated within the ranks of the longshoremen who loaded the ships with squared timber. These men exposed themselves to considerable danger in return for little pay, circumstances which ultimately led them to form the Quebec Ship Labourers Benevolent Society in 1862. [15] They briefly went on strike in 1866, paralyzing the timber trade, but their lot was ultimately determined by market factors that eliminated their jobs. With the decline of the timber trade the English-speaking population of Quebec City fell by 15 % between 1861 and 1871. As Arthur Lower has noted, "When the trade declined, there was a great outpouring to other parts of the continent... The result was a heavy decline in the influence and the numbers of the English-speaking population of Quebec [City]." [16]

For the unskilled English-speaking labourers of Montreal, by contrast, leaving was seen as less of an

---

14. J-P Kesteman, "Les travailleurs à la construction du chemin de fer dans la région de Sherbrooke", *Revue d'histoire de l'Amérique française*, XXXI (1978).

15. J.I. Cooper, "The Quebec Ship Labourers' Benevolent Society", *Canadian Historical Review*, XXX (1949), pp. 336-343.

16. Arthur R.M. Lower, *Great Britain's Woodyard* (Montreal, 1973), p. 228.

option. As the empire of the English-speaking elite expanded, employment prospects arose, albeit in jobs that were not particularly well-paying. Nevertheless, as many jobs as could be found were required by families which could not have survived on a single wage. In 1871, 94 % of the Irish families of the Ste-Anne ward (in the vicinity of the Lachine Canal) had at least one child over 11 years of age in the labour force, and when younger children did not prove too much of a burden the mother of the family also frequently found herself employed outside the home.[17] Women's labour expressed itself not only in the form of factory work, but also as daughters were sent to serve as live-in maids for the English-speakers discussed in the first section of this chapter. In this regard, being English-speaking proved a benefit as few matrons of the St-Antoine district were willing to be inconvenienced by hiring a French-speaking girl.[18] Accordingly, families from the canal district had one less mouth to feed as well as the earnings of their daughter to keep the family economy afloat.

As one can imagine, the energies of the English-speaking labourers of Montreal were usually too taken up by mere survival to contemplate the formation of unions. In any event, these workers were in no position to press their demands upon employers, given the meager skills they possessed. Some examples of labour militancy could be found, however, among the Irish canal workers. There were confrontations between workers and their employers at the Rideau Canal in 1827 and at the Beauharnois Canal in 1843. The most spectacular of these confrontations took place, also in 1843, at the Lachine Canal where 1,300 workers, nearly all Irish, went on strike not only to protest wage

---

17. Bradbury, "The Family Economy".
18. Suzanne Cross, "The Neglected Majority", *Social History*, VI (1973), pp. 202-223.

Monument to the Irish immigrants erected by the Irish workmen on the Victoria Bridge (Public Archives of Canada, C-44482)

View of the farm of P.H. Gosse, Eastern Townships, 1837 (Public Archives of Canada, C-84444)

reductions but also the order that wages had to be spent at the company store.[19] None of these strikes lasted very long, and when the construction work was finished the labourers either moved on to other parts of the continent or settled in to form part of the large pool of unskilled labourers that existed within both the English and French-speaking populations of Montreal by 1867.

3. Farmers

In terms of their absolute numbers, farmers formed the largest occupational grouping among pre-Confederation English speakers. In 1871, 52.8 % of all English speakers were farmers, while the figure was only slightly higher, 56.1 %, for French speakers.[20] But while farming may have occupied a similar place within the occupational structure of the two linguistic groups, some historians have claimed that there were substantial differences in the manner in which English and French-speaking farmers utilized their land. To historians such as Fernand Ouellet, for instance, "two types of agriculture existed in Quebec. The one, traditional and French Canadian, occupied the masses; the other progressive and British, was supported by the British and the French Canadian elite." To support his case Ouellet quoted the president of one agricultural society who observed: "The fundamental principle of British farming is the improvement of the soil according to the best established systems... The French Canadian system, on the contrary, involves the principle (if one wishes to call it such) of soil deterioration."[21] Ouellet's view has received support from fellow histo-

19. H.C. Pentland, "The Lachine Strike of 1843", *Canadian Historical Review*, XXIX (1948), pp. 255-277.

20. See Table 3.1.

21. Ouellet, *Economic and Social History*, pp. 468-469.

rians Jean Hamelin and Yves Roby. They found that "le rendement des terres et des animaux est-il plus élevé dans les Cantons de l'Est que dans les paroisses canadiennes-françaises." They gave the example of the English-speaking farmers of one township where each cow allowed the production of nearly 60 pounds of butter. By contrast, they pointed to the parish of St-Denis where an average of only 16 pounds was produced in 1851.[22]

By placing the English-speaking farmer upon a pedestal and by denigrating the practices of French speakers, Ouellet, Hamelin and Roby provided themselves with little opportunity to consider the unsuccessful English farmer or the French farmer who made great strides in improving his land. Nor did they provide very careful explanations of why the observed differences might have existed. To Ouellet it was essentially a question of *mentalité* that allowed "English-speaking producers of all categories [to fare] better than the French-speaking."[23] But what did it mean "to fare better"? This was precisely the question raised by economists Frank Lewis and Marvin McInnis in an analysis of the state of Quebec agriculture in 1851. They assumed that the "better" farmer was the more efficient farmer, and they pointed out that efficiency had to be considered in terms of the output of the farmer in relation to the labour, land and capital with which he had to work. Their analysis of the census data led them to conclude that "the English in Lower Canada really were not better farmers than were the French."[24] Therefore, the English-speaking farmer may have produced an output of a higher value on an acre

---

22. Jean Hamelin et Yves Roby, *Histoire économique du Québec, 1851-96* (Montreal, 1971), p. 7.

23. Ouellet, *Lower Canada*, p. 180.

24. Frank Lewis and Marvin McInnis, "The Efficiency of the French Canadian Farmer in the Nineteenth Century", *Journal of Economic History*, XL (1980), p. 514.

of land than did his French-speaking counterpart, but this was due to such factors as better land or greater capital.

A more concrete comparison of English and French farmers within a given part of the colony has been provided by historian J.I. Little. He looked at two townships within the county of Compton between 1851 and 1870 and found that "the French Canadians concentrated upon the same major products as the anglophones, but their crop yields were not as high."[25] Little attributed this difference to the fact that French-Canadian farms tended to be much smaller than those owned by English speakers. With larger holdings the English were able to specialize in a variety of cash crops in addition to feeding their families, and with this cash even further progress could be achieved. The French farms remained small as newcomers were constantly moving into the region, while consolidation was possible among the English whose numbers decreased, particularly during the 1860s. The Scottish population of Winslow Township declined by 10 % during the 1860s, while for the region as a whole the decline in the English-speaking population during the decade was 13 %. The ability of the English to head off "to greener pastures [to the] south and west" allowed those who remained to have greater resources at their disposal than were possessed by the less mobile French Canadians.[26] On the farms of Quebec, as had been the case in the cities, a variety of circumstances provided certain advantages for English speakers that were not always available to their French-speaking counterparts.

---

25. J.I. Little, "The Social and Economic Development of Settlers in Two Quebec Townships, 1851-70", *Canadian Papers in Rural History*, I (1978), p. 98.

26. *Ibid.*

Lumberjacks in the Ottawa Valley
(Public Archives of Canada, C-22036)

4. Fishermen and Lumbermen

Not all English speakers living outside the two major cities were full time farmers. There were also those who secured at least part of their living from the sea or from the forests of Quebec. In the former category, most prominent were the English-speaking fishermen of the Gaspé. In 1861 one-quarter of all the residents of the region were English-speaking, and most were scattered among the various outports along the coast. These fishermen were subject to the difficulties imposed by the "truck system". In this system the individual fisherman gained credit from the local merchant for the upcoming season upon particularly onerous terms. The local merchant was usually an agent for one of the few commercial houses which monopolized the region's trade. The most important of these houses was that of Charles Robin and Company, established in the area shortly after the Conquest. Robin and most of the other important merchants in the regional economy were from Jersey in the Channel Islands. These men occupied a curious position within Quebec society for they were British and Protestant, and yet usually had French as their mother tongue.

While their social origins may have placed them in an anomalous position, the Jersey merchants were in complete control of the local economy. They extended credit to a fisherman on the basis that he would sell his entire catch to them at the end of the season, thus removing the opportunity for the fishermen to seek the best price and allowing the merchant to depress prices so as to keep the fisherman in a dependent state. In the event that the debt could not be repaid at the end of the season, the Robin Company would compel the borrower to repair its ships during the winter.[27] Not surprisingly, these English speakers sought to lighten their burden through farming or lumbering, but neither usually permitted escape from the truck system.

The lot of the English speakers who worked in the lumber camps of the Ottawa Valley was similarly unattractive. These camps employed numerous Irishmen who had been drawn to the region by the prospect of work in the building of the Rideau Canal between 1819 and 1834. When the construction was completed the Irish streamed into the lumber camps seeking employment and coming into conflict with French speakers who desired the same jobs. On the Ontario side of the river this competition resulted in the violence of the Shiners' riots of the 1830s, while on the Quebec side such conflict became a matter of concern to local officials.[28] These lumbermen, like their counterparts in the Gaspé outports, earned little for their labour. However, they were able to gain release from their situation

---

27. The same conditions also had to be endured by English speakers living on the lower north shore of the St.Lawrence. See F.W. Remiggi, "Persistence of Ethnicity: A Study of Social and Spatial Boundaries on the Eastern Lower North Shore, 1820-1970", M.A. Thesis, Memorial University, 1975.

28. Michael Cross, "The Shiners' War", *Canadian Historical Review*, LIV (1973), pp. 1-26.

in the pre-Confederation period. With the decline of the timber trade that had such a devastating effect upon Quebec City, the need for large numbers of labourers in the forests of the Ottawa Valley was drastically reduced by the 1860s. As was the case with other English speakers who found economic prospects unappealing, a certain number of these Irishmen probably left Quebec, while others found the means to occupy farms in the region. Indeed, by .1871 Pontiac County was overwhelmingly made up of Irish settlers, nearly all of whom listed farming as their primary occupation, although they might still have supplemented their incomes by occasionally labouring in the forests. The lasting contribution of these people who stayed in the region lies in the fact that Pontiac was the only county in the province still to have an English-speaking majority in 1981.

5. Conclusion

The information that is available regarding the role of English speakers in the Quebec economy prior to 1867 is far more rudimentary than that which exists for the late twentieth century. For instance, by the 1980s there was census information that indicated that the disparities in the incomes of English and French-speaking Quebecers were caused almost entirely by a small number of people at the very top of the economic ladder. Below this elite there was essentially no difference between English and French wage earners.[29] The data do not exist to draw such conclusions for the pre-Confederation period, but there are reasons to believe that a similar situation existed. Prior to 1867 there was an English-speaking elite with substantial wealth and power, but beneath this elite was an English-speaking population which was by 1871 divided

29. Jac-André Boulet, *Language and Earnings in Montreal* (Ottawa, 1980).

among various occupations as was the French majority. Earlier in the pre-Confederation period there had been a larger number of highly skilled craftsmen, but their importance decreased under the weight of industrialization. The bulk of the urban population was made up of families that had to worry about survival. In rural Quebec the English and the French contested the jobs available in the lumber camps and shared the miseries of the truck system in the Gaspé. As farmers, the English were no more efficient than the French, and their greater wealth is open to question. In terms of their role in the economy, English-speaking Quebecers constituted a diverse population.

SELECT BIBLIOGRAPHY

Bradbury, Bettina. "The Family Economy and Work in an Industrializing City", CHA Papers, 1979.

Creighton, Donald. *Empire of the St. Lawrence.* Toronto, 1956.

Little, J.I. "The Social and Economic Development of Settlers in Two Quebec Townships, 1851-70", *Canadian Papers in Rural History*, I (1978), 89-111.

Lower, A.R.M. *Great Britain's Woodyard.* Montreal, 1973.

Ouellet, Fernand. *Economic and Social History of Quebec, 1760-1850.* Ottawa, 1980.

Pentland, H.C. *Labour and Capital in Canada.* Toronto, 1981.

Tulchinsky, Gerald. *The River Barons.* Toronto, 1977.

IV

Ethnicity, Religion and Region

Economic circumstances determined the material basis for the lives of the quarter-million English speakers living in Quebec in 1867. There were also other factors, however, which influenced the way in which these English speakers related to each other and to the French majority. Most important among these factors was religion. While Quebecers of the late twentieth century are obsessed by issues related to language, in the pre-Confederation period, and even well into the 1900s, religion was a crucial factor dividing Quebecers. The central place of religion was given constitutional status as the BNA Act recognized a school system that was divided along denominational lines, and it is generally accepted that religion was an important force in the lives of Quebec's French-speaking Catholics. But what is less well known is that religion also had an important role to play in English-speaking Quebec.

The importance of religion in the lives of the minority is often obscured by the assumption that all English speakers were Protestants, when in fact nearly one-third were Catholics.[1] Accordingly, Catholics made up the most important religious group within the English-speaking population since the Protestants were splintered among thirty-four denominations. Throughout the pre-Confederation period, the English-speaking Catholics tried to find a place for themselves within a society whose most powerful figures were either French Catholics or English Protestants. As for the latter group, it alternated between tearing itself apart over internal differences and working as a unit to confront the powers of the Catholic hierarchy. In these ways religion occupied a central place in the lives of English speakers.

English Quebecers were further divided, however, by ethnic or national ties that frequently cut across religious lines. As Table 4.1 indicates, over half of all English speakers were of Irish origin in 1871, while only 29 % of English speakers were Catholics. Evidently there were large numbers of Irish Protestants in the colony, just as there were Catholic minorities within the Scottish and English populations. These ethnic ties

---

1. Determining the percentage of English speakers who were Catholic in the pre-Confederation period is no easy matter. While English speakers have been defined as Quebecers of British origin during most of this period, there is no published census data providing cross references between religion and ethnicity. Throughout this chapter certain assumptions have been made so as to estimate the number of English speakers in each of the major religions. First, it was assumed that all Protestants were British so as to allow the use of the census data regarding specific Protestant denominations. Further assumptions were required, however, to determine the number of English-speaking Catholics. By assuming that all Quebecers of French origin were Catholic, it was then possible to subtract the number of Protestants in a given area from the number who were of British origin to arrive at an estimate of the English Catholic population. These calculations for the province of Quebec in 1871 are listed below.

Population of British Origin	243,041
— Protestant Population	−171,686
English-Catholic Population	71,355 (29 %)

were important for a people who were rarely more
than a generation removed from another land. In 1844,
for instance, roughly half of the English-speaking
population had been born outside Canada. Some could
directly trace their roots back to various parts of Britain, while others had ties with families which had
come to Quebec from Britain via the American co-
lonies/states to the south. Occasionally, these ethnic
ties superseded those of religion, as was the case in
the early history of the St. Patrick's Society which
united all of the Irish of Montreal regardless of religion. In time, however, religion won out and two
organizations, one for each of the two major religious
groups, were formed. While not ignoring the importance of ethnicity, this chapter will give greater emphasis to the force of religion. The first section will
discuss the lives of English-speaking Protestants while
the second will deal with their Catholic counterparts.

TABLE 4.1

Religion and Ethnicity
of English-Speaking Quebecers, 1871

RELIGION		ETHNIC ORIGIN	
Catholic	29 %	Irish	51 %
Anglican	26 %	English	29 %
Methodist	19 %	Scottish	20 %
Presbyterian	14 %		
Baptist	4 %		
Other non-Catholic sects	8 %		

Source: *Census of Canada.*

A third section of the chapter will examine the
regional concerns that provided a further source of
division among English speakers. To be sure, ethnic
and religious differences among the English-speaking
residents of any region hindered the development of

strong regional identities. At the same time, however, the dominance of certain groups in particular regions contributed to the development of those strong regional identities that did emerge. In the pre-Confederation era, for instance, the Eastern Townships stood out as a region where residents had strong ties with the United States. Accordingly, while 35 % of all English speakers in 1851 had been born in Britain, the figure was only 22 % for the English speakers of the Eastern Townships. That region also stood out in terms of its religious composition, as only 11 % of the English-speaking population was Catholic in 1871, well below the figure for all English speakers in Quebec. By and large, however, these ethnic and religious influences were more of a hindrance than a help in fostering regional identities among people who had both a common language and certain common concerns based upon local economic circumstances. Nevertheless, there were moments in which English speakers in any given region did act as one in response to particular regional concerns. Such regional responses were particularly important to the pre-Confederation population which, as the following table indicates, had not yet been concentrated in Montreal.

In the three sections that follow, the various ethnic, religious and regional identities of the pre-Confederation English-speaking population will be explored. Particular emphasis will be placed upon the educational system, whose early evolution gave rise to some of the most important divisions within the minority. Similarly, special attention will be reserved for the BNA Act, several of whose provisions reflected the nature of these various divisions in 1867.

TABLE 4.2

Regional Distribution
of English-Speaking Quebecers, 1871

REGION	% OF ALL ENGLISH SPEAKERS IN QUEBEC
Eastern Townships	32 %
Montreal	27 %
Ottawa Valley	15 %
Quebec City	9 %
Gaspé	5 %
Not included in other categories	12 %

Source: *Census of Canada.*

1. The Protestants

For the British officials who were plotting the
future course for Quebec in the aftermath of the conquest, Quebec was not simply to be a Protestant land,
but more specifically, an Anglican one. The Church of
England was the established church at home, which
was to say that it received the financial support of the
State. There was little question in 1760 that it would
have the same status in Quebec, and the Proclamation
of 1763 unambiguously declared that the church would
be "established 'both in principle and practice' with
government support under the direction of the Bishop
of London."[2] But just as the British were slow in
implementing other aspects of their avowed policy of
anglicization in the face of a French-Catholic majority
whose favour was desired, they were also lax in the
"establishment" of the Church of England in Quebec.

---

2. John S. Moir, *The Church in the British Era* (Toronto, 1972), p. 38.

However, following the American Revolution the resolve of British policymakers strengthened in terms of actively promoting the establishment of the Church of England. There was a feeling that the Americans had been allowed to stray from the fold, in part, through their adherence to a variety of religions, Methodism in particular, which encouraged a lack of respect for monarchical authority. So as to avoid such a situation in Quebec, the Constitutional Act of 1791 contained provisions to give substance to the promises of support for the Church of England. One clause stipulated that funds were to be made available "for the support and maintenance of a Protestant clergy" by setting aside one seventh of all lands in the newly opened townships for this purpose. A second clause instructed the governor "to constitute and erect within every township one or more Parsonage or Rectory" by providing "as much land as might seem expedient."[3]

Much to the dismay of successive Anglican bishops, however, these fine sounding intentions translated into little concrete support in the face of the realities of Quebec where the co-operation of another church was more important to British officials. These policymakers never resolved the problem as to how the good faith of the Catholic hierarchy might be preserved if the Anglican church were really established. Accordingly, while the Anglican clergy in Upper Canada became a powerful political force, in Lower Canada similar political influence was absent. In Upper Canada support by the State for the Church of England, particularly in the form of the clergy reserves, became one of the major political issues leading up to the Rebellion of 1837. By contrast, in Quebec the issue inspired no particular passion. The lands were of little value until the 1820s, and by then there was a serious competitor for these funds in the Church of

---

3. *Ibid.*, p. 61.

Scotland. The Anglicans in Quebec were never strong
enough to discredit completely the pretentions of the
Presbyterians, and they were forced to accept a certain
sharing of State support in the 1840s. In the 1850s, the
clergy reserves passed from the scene in Lower Canada almost unnoticed, as all attention was focused upon
the simultaneous abolition of seigneurial tenure.

This lack of official support did not prevent the
Anglican hierarchy from claiming an ascendant role
within English-speaking Quebec, an attitude that led
to conflict with the other Protestant denominations.
This assumption of importance was particularly evident in the role played by the first Anglican bishop,
Jacob Mountain, in the establishment of the province's
first system of public education. The Royal Institution
for the Advancement of Learning (RIAL) was formed
by the government of Lower Canada in 1801, but
remained largely a dead letter in terms of the actual
establishment of schools until 1818. Mountain was the
Institution's first principal, and most of its trustees
were Anglicans. The Institution was to provide State
support for schools that had been begun by local
initiative, and it even made concessions to the French-
Catholic majority so as to allow curés to inspect the
operations of RIAL schools. In spite of such commitments the Catholic hierarchy remained sceptical, a fact
that is well reported in most histories of Quebec education.[4] Less well known, however, is the opposition
that also surfaced from other Protestant denominations. As Nathan Mair has noted: "The Royal Institution was never able to rid itself of its English and
Anglican image... No place was given among [its]
trustees to official representation from the Church of
Scotland. Some Presbyterians must have noticed that

---

4. See, for instance, Louis-Philippe Audet, *Histoire de l'enseignement au
   Québec* (Montreal, 1971).

only Anglican catechisms were available for distribution in the schools; Methodists, no doubt, felt rejected because their requests for the use of school buildings for their meetings were commonly denied."[5]

Because of these various inter-denominational struggles, no coherent system of education emerged before the Rebellion of 1837. For many English-speaking Protestants education was directly provided by their church. The Anglicans, the Presbyterians and the Methodists all operated schools of their own during the pre-1837 period in the same way that they provided charitable services for their poor. But even the provision of these services was frequently hindered by the intra-denominational squabbles that further splintered the English-speaking population. No Protestant denomination was more divided than the Presbyterians who were distributed among six different "sub-sects" in the 1871 census. These divisions were the product of various doctrinal, national and class interests.

In Quebec, as in Scotland, the theological issue that divided Presbyterians pertained to the links between the Church of Scotland and the State. Upon several occasions these controversies from Britain spilled over into Quebec causing schisms. Proclaiming its independence from the State, the Free Church was formed in the 1840s, shortly after which deputations from Scotland were sent to Montreal and Quebec City to gain support there. These doctrinal conflicts were joined by ethnic and class antagonisms to divide Quebec's Presbyterians even further. Such divisions were evident in the establishment of the various Presbyterian churches in Montreal. The first, St. Gabriel's, was founded in 1792 and soon became the place of worship of the Scottish fur barons. In 1803 the more humble

5. Nathan Mair, *Quest for Quality in the Protestant Public Schools of Quebec* (Quebec, 1980), p. 16.

members of St. Gabriel's, together with some American merchants, set off to establish their own church, St. Peter's, which itself lost part of its adherents when the American Presbyterian Church was formed in 1822.

American influences also provided a divisive force in the affairs of the Methodist church. The Methodists were concentrated to a great degree in the Eastern Townships and the Ottawa Valley, two regions that had largely been settled by Americans in the decades leading up to the War of 1812. These Americans came with a strong opposition to close ties between church and State, and these values caused them some difficulty when the war began. So awkward was the position of Americans in the Huntingdon region near the American border that many returned to the south. In religious terms the war cut off the supply of preachers from the States, and British Wesleyan Methodism, with its less radical rejection of the ties between church and State, began to take hold. Still, in 1861 the majority of Quebec's Methodists belonged to non-Wesleyan sects and upheld the traditions of "militant evangelism, circuit rider democracy and lay participation in church management."[6]

These various conflicts both within and between the Protestant denominations reflected the central role of religion for all pre-Confederation Quebecers. Religion provided a major source of one's identity, and English-speaking Quebecers were prolific in establishing churches that might reflect their diverse interests. By 1871 there were 429 Protestant churches in the province. This figure represented 41 % of all churches in Quebec even though Protestants accounted for only 14 % of the province's population.

There is a danger, however, in overemphasizing these divisions, for in the three decades leading up to

6. Moir, p. 165.

Confederation there was considerable evidence of in-creased co-operation both between members of the same denomination and between the denominations themselves. In terms of intra-denominational unity, most Presbyterians in Quebec formed part of the Cana-dian Presbyterian Church established in 1861, while the Methodists had achieved a similar unification by 1874. Even more significant for the history of English-speaking Quebec, however, was the evidence of inter-denominational co-operation in the sphere of education. In the aftermath of the Rebellion of 1837, education in Lower Canada was in complete disarray. Prior to 1837 there had been several types of schools receiving various forms of assistance from the govern-ment, but this support ended with the rebellions. The time was ripe for the creation of a new educational structure for the province. To British colonial officials such as Lord Durham the cherished hope was the establishment of a single, common school system for both of the Canadas so that the assimilation of the French might be hastened. The School Act of 1841 established a single educational system for the now united Canada. There was to be a single Superinten-dent of Education who would provide grants to sub-sidize local schools.

This system proved to be impractical given the very different traditions of the two Canadas, and by the mid-1840s Ontario and Quebec had formed sepa-rate bureaucracies. However, there was one aspect of the 1841 law that persisted until the 1980s and which contributed greatly to the coalescing of Quebec's En-glish-speaking Protestants. The 1841 act established common schools open to all students regardless of religion. At the same time, however, it also allowed for the creation of dissentient schools. The religious mi-nority within a given school district, if it were to feel ill at ease sharing schools with the majority, was free to establish schools of its own without any loss of public support. Once this provision was introduced the concept of common schools was for all intents and purposes dead. Given the religious passions of the time, why would any religious group choose to remain in the minority if it could have a school of its own? Outside of Montreal and Quebec City (where different rules existed), only 190 of the 3,712 schools in operation in 1867 were dissentient schools. This should not be seen, however, as a willingness on the part of Catholics and Protestants to work together. Rather it was a comment upon the geographical separation of Catholics and Protestants within Quebec.

In fact, the bi-denominational nature of Quebec education became even more evident during the 1840s and 1850s. For instance, when an 1845 act established the structure for the schools of Montreal and Quebec City no reference was made to common and dissentient schools. Instead, in each city two distinct corporations were to be formed, one to look after Catholic education and the other to attend to Protestant concerns. Similarly, when the Council of Public Instruction was formed in 1859 to set policy on educational matters, the seats on the council were earmarked for members who represented one denomination or the other. As Nathan Mair notes, "Within a few years [after 1859] it was found to be convenient to allow informal 'Catholic' and 'Protestant' committees of the Council to choose certain texts for schools of their respective denomination which did not necessarily require the approval of the whole Council. This was the first step in the formulation of official separate curricula for Catholic and Protestant schools."[7]

Given this institutional framework the various Protestant sects had little choice but to work together. There was nothing in the school laws that gave control

---

7. Mair, p. 21.

J.W. Dawson
(Public Archives of Canada, C-49822)

American Presbyterian Church,
Montreal
(Public Archives of Canada, C-G5419)

to individual denominations, making co-operation essential. Historian John Moir has also attributed this co-operation to the weakening, by the 1840s, of the ties between the Canadian churches and their British counterparts, thus removing the "old world's" conflicts from the scene. A further bone of contention was removed by the 1850s with the end of discussion regarding State support for an established church.[8] In the Quebec context, this co-operation also proved to be essential in the face of a reinvigorated Catholic church that was trying to expand its authority in the aftermath of the Rebellion of 1837. The so-called Catholic revival was spearheaded by Bishop Ignace Bourget of Montreal who worked energetically to increase the number of priests in the province. He succeeded in boosting the number from 500 in 1840 to 2100 by 1880.[9] In the face of this growing Catholic power, the Protestants had to unite so as to secure specific changes in the School Act, particularly those that increased the power of dissentient school commissioners to control their taxes and property.[10]

This co-operation which was forged by the "dissentient" clause was also visible in other spheres. In terms of providing social services the various Protestant denominations of Montreal united to establish the Protestant Home of Industry in 1863 and the Mackay Institute for the Protestant Deaf Mutes and the Blind in 1868. This new spirit of co-operation was equally to be found in McGill University's new charter of 1852, by which it was to be a Protestant institution, but one

---

8. Moir, p. 173.

9. Louis-Edmond Hamelin, "Évolution numérique séculaire du clergé catholique dans le Québec", *Recherches sociographiques*, II (1961), pp. 189-241.

10. See Keith Hunte, "The Development of a System of Education in Canada East, 1841-67", M.A. Thesis, McGill University, 1962.

without denominational ties. McGill's principal, J.W.
Dawson, championed this inter-denominational approach, and was given an even greater opportunity to
advance it in the years leading up to Confederation.

If the increased assertiveness of the Catholic
church had given rise to co-operation among the Protestants, then the movement towards Confederation
between 1864 and 1867 solidified that spirit. It was
clear from the beginning of negotiations that education
would become a provincial responsibility, and the Protestants reacted to the danger that a Catholic-
dominated provincial government might pose to their
educational interests. Therefore, in 1864 Dawson and
others formed the Association for the Promotion and
Protection of the Educational Interests of the Protestants of Lower Canada. The Quebec Resolutions,
which contained the essence of the Confederation arrangement and which were to be submitted to each
colonial legislature, were drafted in 1864. They
stipulated that education would be under provincial
jurisdiction, but that all rights enjoyed by the religious
minority at the time of Confederation would be guaranteed. To Dawson and his friends, given the wording
of the educational clause, there was an incentive to
have the extent of Protestant rights increased prior to
Confederation. In particular, they wanted the creation
of a separate Protestant bureaucracy headed by a superintendent of Protestant education. These demands
were embodied in the Langevin Bill which was presented to the legislature of the united Canadas in 1866.
The bill was defeated, however, and when the BNA
Act came into force on 1 July 1867 it was without all
the guaranteed rights that the Protestants would have
liked. Article 93 of the Act granted, as had the Quebec
Resolutions, existing rights; but to many Protestants
these were not sufficient.

Principal Dawson and his associates cared little about the educational rights of English-speaking Catholics in the new federation. Given the importance of religion at the time, they fought for denominational interests and showed no concern for their co-linguists who professed Catholicism. Even the unity that existed among Protestants was fragile, and emerged only because of the specific circumstances of the decades leading up to Confederation. A certain "common front" of Quebec's Protestants had emerged by 1867, but this did not conceal the divisions that still existed between denominations. For instance, Anglicans had in the 1840s established their own university, Bishop's, in the Eastern Townships. In the same region, there were also Methodists with close ties with the States to the south and Scottish immigrants with ties with Presbyterianism. On a day-to-day basis these religious and ethnic divisions still played a key role in people's lives; only on larger political issues could the hatchet be buried to advance certain common Protestant concerns.

2. English-Speaking Catholics

John Moir has described English-speaking Catholics as having occupied the position of a "double minority" in pre-Confederation Canada.[11] They belonged to a linguistic minority within a religion that represented only a minority of the British North American population. Within Quebec, however, the situation was somewhat more complicated as Catholics constituted a majority of the population. Accordingly, the English-speaking Catholics of Quebec had to confront not only a Protestant population that had little sym-

---

11. J.S. Moir, "The Problem of Double Minority: Some Reflections on the Development of the English-Speaking Catholic Church in Canada in the Nineteenth Century", *Social History*, VII (1971), pp. 53-67.

pathy for them, but also a Catholic church dominated by French speakers and, especially after 1837, anxious to assert its political power.

Given the evolution of Quebec society along denominational lines, there was relatively little opportunity for interaction on any institutional level between English-speaking Catholics and their Protestant counterparts. One exception to this rule came in the initial constitution of Montreal's St. Patrick's Society in 1834 as an institution representing all of the Irish, Catholic and Protestant alike. While there were people of Scottish or English origin among the province's English-speaking Catholic population, by the 1830s the Irish made up the vast majority. Had the St. Patrick's Society maintained its non-denominational status, this would have constituted an important bridge between Catholics and Protestants. However, in the midst of the polarization of Quebec's religious groups in the decades leading up to Confederation, the St. Patrick's Society was transformed. In 1856 the Irish Protestants abandoned it to form the Irish Protestant Benevolent Society, thus leaving the St. Patrick's Society to the Catholics.

By contrast, contacts between the Irish Catholics and Quebec's French-Catholic population were much more frequent. This was to be expected, given not only the importance of religion but also the similarity of economic experience noted in the previous chapter. It is difficult, however, to characterize the nature of the relationship between the French and the Irish Catholics. On the personal level there were indications of goodwill between the two groups evident in the marriages that frequently occurred. As a result of these Irish-French marriages, 15 % of all Quebecers of Irish origin had French as their mother tongue when such information was first reported in 1931. For all Quebecers of British origin in 1931 the figure was only 9 %.

The other side of the coin, however, was that personal relations were often strained between the Irish and the French owing to their competition for similar jobs near the bottom of the occupational structure. The previous chapter described the Irish-French conflict that constituted the Shiners' War in the Ottawa Valley. Similarly, the Irish and the French clashed over the latter's role as scab labourers during the strikes at the Beauharnois and Lachine canals in the 1840s. In the aftermath of the Lachine strike, the canal's contractor tried to undercut the position of the Irish by employing French speakers who would work for less. The consequence was described by one newspaper: "A number of [French] Canadians were assailed by a party of Irishmen with stones and driven off the Canal. One man received a severe blow on the head from a missile, and all were so much intimidated so as to render it unlikely they [would] return." [12]

Indications of both friendship and hostility were also evident in the dealings between the French and the Irish on the institutional level. On the one hand, there are numerous accounts regarding the kindness accorded to the Irish by Catholic institutions, particularly upon their large-scale arrival in the 1840s. In the migrations of 1847 roughly 25,000 died at the quarantine station on Grosse Isle. Among the priests who tended the Irish was the future Cardinal Taschereau, while at Montreal the Sulpicians did all they could to provide care and schooling for the Irish. [13] In other cases, however, the attitude of the Catholic hierarchy towards the Irish was totally lacking in charity. There was a case in 1823, for instance, when Bishop Plessis of Quebec discussed the Irish in the following terms: "Here the Irish are numerous. They do not bring priests with them. Those whom they have brought

12. Pentland, *Labour and Capital*, p. 120.
13. Brian Young, *George-Etienne Cartier* (Montreal, 1981), p. 104.

St. Patrick's Church, Montreal
(Public Archives of Canada,
C-2058)

The Lachine Canal Labourers' Strike
(Public Archives of Canada,
C-67503)

would be the dregs of the Irish clergy as [the Irish immigrants] are the scum of the population."[14]

Rhetoric aside, the major bone of contention in both Quebec City and Montreal between the Irish population and the Catholic hierarchy pertained to the establishment of distinctive Irish parishes within the two cities. The Irish sought the establishment of national parishes that would be defined by ethnicity or language, and not merely by geography as was usually the case. In Quebec City, for instance, the issue was not the construction of a church for the Irish, as St. Patrick's was dedicated in 1833 thanks to the efforts of the community's well-to-do elements. The problem was gaining recognition of St. Patrick's as the parish church for all English-speaking Catholics in the city. The securing of this status, which was only achieved in 1856, would guarantee the provision of a wide array of services in English for Catholics throughout the city.[15] In Montreal the battle for the establishment of an English-Catholic parish was even more arduous since the opponent was Bishop Bourget. St. Patrick's Church was opened in Montreal in 1847, but it did not receive the status of a parish church until 1873, and then only after the intervention of the Pope. To clerics such as Bishop Bourget, who had been responsible for the Catholic revival in Quebec after 1837, the danger to Catholicism came not only from Protestants but also from English-speaking Catholics. Bourget believed that the survival of Catholicism in Quebec was closely bound up with the French language; as long as Quebec's Catholics were French they would have a linguistic shield from the English-speaking world of North American Protestantism. In this view of affairs the Irish were considered a potential threat. If they were

---

14. William Nolte, "The Irish in Canada, 1815-1867", Ph.D. Thesis, University of Maryland, 1975.

15. O'Gallagher, p. 101.

given encouragement to live as English-speaking Catholics in Montreal, there would be explicit approval of interaction between French Catholics and English speakers. This breakdown in linguistic purity could only lead in the long run to religious disaster. Accordingly, the Irish had to struggle to gain a parish of their own, and they also had to fight to secure fair treatment within the Catholic schools of Montreal.

With the establishment of the Quebec educational system in the 1840s Catholic school commissions were formed for the two major cities. Within the Montreal Catholic School Commission (MCSC) the early experience of the Irish was hardly positive. Since all members of the MCSC were appointed, the Irish were in no position to be guaranteed a seat on the board. Indeed, from 1845 to 1860 the Irish held a seat on the six-member board for only five years. In the light of this poor representation there were complaints, particularly in the post-Confederation period, about the facilities provided for English Catholic education.[16]

Outside of the two cities the Irish Catholics did little better in a system where dissentient schools could only be formed on the basis of religion. Schools therefore tended to be either English-Protestant or French-Catholic. In the years leading up to Confederation there were a few Irish leaders calling for the right to dissent on the basis of language as well as religion. Given the structure of pre- Confederation Quebec society, it is little wonder that their requests fell on deaf ears.[17] There was nothing in the educational provisions of the BNA Act to recognize the peculiar position of Quebec's English-speaking Catholics.

---

16. See D.S. Cross, "The Irish in Montreal, 1867-96", M.A. Thesis, McGill University, 1969.
17. Hunte, p. 171.

3. Regional Identities

Within each of the regions of Quebec where English speakers were present in significant numbers, one could find evidence of the sort of ethnic and religious divisions noted in the first two sections of this chapter. So important were these divisions that they often led to the physical separation of English speakers of different backgrounds. For instance, in the Ottawa Valley Irish Catholics were dominant upstream from Hull, while Scottish and Irish Protestants were the mainstays of the English-speaking population downstream. In the Eastern Townships, Stanstead County had, at the time of Confederation, an English-speaking majority that was primarily of English origin, while in Compton County certain townships were dominated by Scots. Similarly, in the Gaspé the different English-speaking groups lived apart from one another.[18]

While ethnic and religious factors had the potential to divide the English speakers of a particular region, they could also foster a certain sense of regional identity, as different groups of English speakers dominated different regions. As Table 4.3 indicates, the Eastern Townships stood out not only because the English-speaking residents of the region had close ties with the States to the south, but also because they were more likely, in 1871, to have been of English origin and Protestant than English speakers in any other part of the province. By contrast, English speakers in the Quebec City area were overwhelmingly Irish and Catholic.

---

18. Jules Bélanger et al., *Histoire de la Gaspésie* (Montréal, 1981).

TABLE 4.3

Ethnicity and Religion of English Speakers
in the Different Regions of Quebec, 1871

	% ENGLISH SPEAKERS BY ETHNIC ORIGIN			% ENGLISH SPEAKERS WHO WERE CATHOLIC
	English	Irish	Scots	
Montreal	25	50	25	37 %
Eastern Townships	43	38	19	11
Ottawa Valley	12	62	26	30
Quebec City	21	69	10	59
Gaspé	33	32	34	35
Quebec	29	51	20	29

Source: *Census of Canada.*

More potent as a source of regional identity, however, were the issues which could transcend ethnic
and religious interests. One such issue was transportation. Throughout the pre-Confederation period the
English speakers who settled outside of Montreal or
Quebec City were drawn together by their isolation.
Their distance from major centres created problems in
securing supplies and sending goods to market. Consequently, in areas such as the Eastern Townships the
need for better transportation facilities was universally
acknowledged, first in the 1820s and 1830s when the
issue was road construction, and later in the 1840s and
1850s when attention was turned to railways. Argu-
ments emerged over the exact route to be followed by
a specific road or railway line, but rarely did people
differ in their belief that better transportation facilities
were needed.

A second and even more potent force in bringing
the English speakers of a region together was the
threat of being greatly outnumbered by the local

TABLE 4.4

Regional Distribution
of English Speakers, 1861-1871

1861	MONT-REAL	EASTERN TOWN-SHIPS	OTTAWA VALLEY	QUEBEC CITY	GASPÉ
A: Regional English-Speaking Pop.	64,531	89,748	34,612	30,656	11,972
A as % of Total English-Speaking Population in Quebec	25	34	13	17	5
A as % of Total Regional Pop.	28	58	64	39	25
1871					
B: Regional English-Speaking Pop.	66,062	77,789	35,669	22,730	11,487
B as % of Total English-Speaking Population in Quebec	27	32	15	9	5
B as % of Total Regional Pop.	27	46	53	29	19

Source: *Census of Canada.*

French-speaking population. As Table 4.4 indicates, English speakers in the Montreal region were thrown further into the minority during the 1860s, while the English speakers of Quebec City experienced an absolute decline in their numbers because of the collapse of the timber trade. Nevertheless, in both cities substantial English-speaking populations remained within a concentrated area so as to allow the perpetuation of various services and institutions. By contrast, in rural Quebec where English speakers were spread out over large areas, demographic changes were greeted with greater concern. In most of these regions the post-Confederation period was marked by the departure of English speakers together with a significant increase in the French-speaking population. These changes threatened the continued existence of English-language services. Accordingly, they encouraged all segments of the remaining English-speaking population to respond in a common fashion. A foreshadowing of these post-Confederation developments was provided by the Eastern Townships in the years leading up to Confederation.

Map of Stanstead County in the Eastern Townships, 1881
(Public Archives of Canada, National Map Collection, 43330)

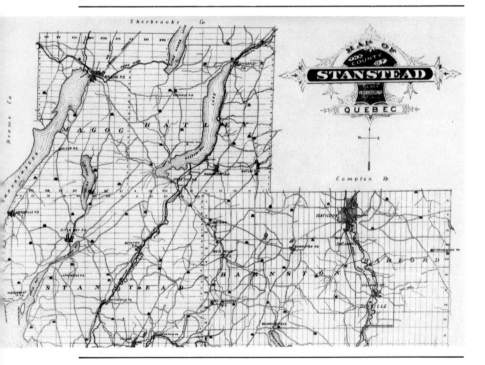

At the start of the 1860s more than one-third of all English speakers lived in the Eastern Townships, and thanks to their efforts the region could boast an English-language university of its own as well as a bank entirely under the control of local English speakers. During the 1860s, however, there was an absolute decline of 13 % in the area's English-speaking population as farmers headed out of the region, and probably out of the province, with few immigrants coming to replace them. Over the same decade the French-speaking population increased significantly with the result that the percentage of the local population that was English-speaking declined from 58 % to 46 %. In the years leading up to the Rebellion of 1837, English-speaking residents of the Gaspé, regardless of origin or religion, had rallied to the idea of the annexation of their region by New Brunswick to counteract the difficulties of being in a minority situation.[19] Similarly, in the Eastern Townships, in the 1860s, there was a widespread consensus that British immigration to the region had to be stepped up so as to lock out the further arrival of French speakers from the seigneurial lands.[20]

When the immigrants from Britain were not forthcoming the Townshippers looked to Confederation as a possible means of securing their interests. Just as English-speaking Protestants used the negotiations leading up to Confederation as a means of bolstering their position in the face of an increasingly aggressive Catholic church, so too did the residents of the Eastern Townships try to secure special consideration before their demographic position deteriorated too badly. Their spokesman was Alexander Galt, who had also

19. *Ibid*.
20. J.I. Little, "Watching the Frontier Disappear: English-Speaking Reaction to French Canadian Colonization in the Eastern Townships, 1844-1890", *Journal of Canadian Studies*, XV (1980-81), pp. 98-103.

tried to steer the ill-fated Langevin Bill through the legislature in 1866 with a view to increasing the educational rights of Quebec's Protestants.

Galt was more successful in championing the interests of Townshippers for he secured the inclusion of Article 80 in the BNA Act. Under this article, the boundaries of twelve provincial ridings (nine in the Eastern Townships and three in the Ottawa Valley) were to remain unaltered unless certain conditions were met. Since the government was seen as having been a major force in the movement of French speakers to the region, there was considerable fear as to what a future government of Quebec might do. Article 80 therefore made the region's ridings immune from change unless a majority of the representatives from the twelve ridings were in agreement with the change. In this way no Quebec government could, for instance, take part of the overwhelmingly French riding of Iberville and attach it to the largely English riding of Missisquoi without observing the rules in Article 80. In the face of a deteriorating situation English-speaking Townshippers rallied together and displayed a regional identity in support of Galt's actions.

4. Conclusion

In this and in the previous chapter the different types of identities possessed by English-speaking Quebecers in the pre-Confederation period have been described. Depending upon the circumstances, different groups of English speakers could be found working together. In their attempt to build a trans-Atlantic economy based at Montreal, that city's business elite worked in isolation from most other English speakers. However, when it came to certain concerns of interest to all Protestants, these businessmen were united with labourers and farmers across the province. When it came to advancing the concerns of the English-speaking residents of the Eastern Townships Irish Catholics in the area were capable of working with those of different ethnic and religious backgrounds; but when it was a question of their specific educational concerns the English- speaking Catholics were on their own.

English-speaking Quebecers were in a position to form these various alliances because of the diversity of the elements that made up the pre-Confederation population. In this chapter certain political issues were discussed so as to observe the interaction of these various English-speaking groups. This discussion will be pursued in the next chapter which offers a more general analysis of the role of English speakers in pre-Confederation politics in Quebec.

SELECT BIBLIOGRAPHY

Bélanger, Jules, et al. *Histoire de la Gaspésie*. Montreal, 1981.

Little, J.I. "Watching the Frontier Disappear: English-Speaking Reaction to French Canadian Colonization in the Eastern Townships, 1844-1890.", *Journal of Canadian Studies*, XV (1980-1), 93-111.

Mair, Nathan. *The Quest for Quality in the Protestant Public Schools of Quebec*. Quebec, 1980.

Moir, John. *The Church in the British Era*. Toronto, 1972.

Price, Lynda. *Introduction to the Social History of Scots in Quebec*. Ottawa, 1981.

V

English-Speaking Quebec and Pre-Confederation Politics

The Rebellions of 1837-8 and the 1980 referendum on sovereignty-association do not at first glance appear to have very much in common. While both were vaguely directed towards the independence of Quebec, the former was an armed insurrection while the latter was a peaceful plebiscite. In terms of the attitude displayed by French and English-speaking Quebecers, however, the two events bear certain similarities. In both cases there was a clear division of opinion within the linguistic majority. In 1837, Louis-Joseph Papineau rallied only a small percentage of French speakers to take up arms, although a larger number were likely sympathetic to his cause. In 1980 the votes were fairly evenly divided between the "yes" and the "no" sides within the French-speaking population. By contrast, there was near unanimity within the English-speaking population in both 1837 and 1980. One historian has found that only 8 % of all Patriotes were English speakers, about equal to the percentage of English speakers who voted "yes" in 1980. [1]

---

1. Jean-Paul Bernard, *Les Rébellions de 1837-38* (Montreal, 1983), p. 323.

Because the events of 1837 and 1980 were dramatic, historians have tended to single them out and to try to draw conclusions from them. In so doing, however, they have wrongly characterized English-speaking Quebecers as a group which generally acted as a bloc on political matters. In the exceptional cases of 1837 and 1980 the threat, however vague, of Quebec's independence brought all of the various English-speaking groups together. Under normal conditions that were less emotionally charged, however, the economic, ethnic, religious and regional divisions noted in the previous chapters were able to take hold. This chapter will emphasize the manner in which the political behaviour of English speakers in the pre-Confederation era reflected the various strains within that population.

1. 1760-1791

During the first thirty years following the Conquest, British officials struggled with little success to find a political system for Quebec that would alienate neither the French majority nor the ever-growing English-speaking minority. The Proclamation of 1763, the first of these attempts, was explicit in its aim of anglicization, but, as we saw in Chapter II, few of the provisions that might have anglicized the colony were ever implemented. Of these provisions, one of the most important was that which would have established an elected assembly in the colony. Given the fact that Catholics were then barred from either voting or holding office, this assembly would have been dominated by the camp followers, and it was consequently never introduced so as not to alienate the French. The Quebec Act of 1774 did not even suggest the introduction of an elected assembly, so that from the Conquest up to 1791 Quebec was ruled by a colonial governor and his hand-picked advisors.

In the absence of elections it is only possible to know the political attitudes of a small percentage of the English-speaking population, Nevertheless, even within this small group there was a clear division of opinion on the issue of colonial rule by the governor and his council. One faction included merchants such as George Allsopp who regularly opposed the governors for their inclination to pander to the French population. The camp followers who came to form the "English Party" energetically battled the governors for political control so as to advance their business interests. For all their efforts, however, the merchants achieved little during these early years aside from the removal of Governor Murray and the harassment of his successor, Guy Carleton. In fact, in terms of the influence that they exercised these merchants were eclipsed by a second faction of English speakers who belonged to what was known as the "French Party". These were the advisors of the governor who sat on his council and who frequently implemented policy which the merchants interpreted as too well disposed towards the French, thus the name "French Party". The English members of this party were almost invariably professional men or office holders who had little in common with the merchants. Typical of these English speakers was Adam Mabane, described by historian A.L. Burt as "the Scot who had been transformed into an upper-class French Canadian. With all the zeal of the convert he became the implacable foe of the whole tribe of English-speaking merchants."[2] Initially trained as a doctor, Mabane came to Canada in 1760 and served in various capacities, most notably as a judge and as a member of the council.

The lack of sympathy shown to the merchants by Mabane and his allies was logical in that they were administrators whose major concern was keeping the

2. Burt, p. 401.

peace in the colony, and this meant appeasing the leaders of French-Canadian society, the clergy and the seigneurs. This division between the French and English parties only made sense, however, as long as the rule of the council continued, for it was the council's right to govern that was at issue. In 1791, a year before the death of Mabane, the Quebec Act was amended and a new and very different political regime was introduced, bringing with it new political divisions within the English-speaking population.

2. 1791-1837

The Constitutional Act of 1791 changed the political role of English Quebecers in a number of ways. First, it rendered the earlier debates between men such as Mabane and Allsopp irrelevant by establishing an elected assembly for the newly created colony of Lower Canada. Had the assembly been formed to represent interests from across the "old province of Quebec" the merchants would have been pleased, as they would have been united with the growing English-speaking population to the west of the Ottawa River. But with the separation of Upper and Lower Canada, the merchants found themselves with an assembly that they could not hope to control. In the first sessions of the legislative assembly of Lower Canada these merchants were over-represented, but it was francophone professionals who soon took charge and who looked to the assembly as the podium from which to advance their own interests.

Just as the colony of Lower Canada was being formed, the economic interests of the merchants were changing. By the turn of the century the fur trade was in decline, and the new staples that were taking the place of furs required facilities that could not be established without government support. As the elected assembly could not function as the vehicle to advance their interests, the merchants looked elsewhere in the new structure of government for sympathy. They found it, ironically, in two bodies whose members were appointed by the governor. The legislative council was the upper house in the legislature of Lower Canada, which had the power both to block disagreeable initiatives from the assembly and to take initiatives of its own. Moreover, the governor made day-to-day decisions based upon advice from men that he appointed to his executive council. On both of these councils the English-speaking merchants held considerable influence. In fact, between 1791 and 1840, 51 % of the members of the legislative council and 69 % of all executive councilors were English-speaking. In the face of the French majority in the assembly, the governor and the merchants were now able to work together amicably.

In the changed circumstances after 1791 the merchants also found themselves politically allied with the office holders against whom they had earlier battled. Fearful that the assembly might usurp the governor's power to make appointments, Adam Mabane's successors had good reason to rally to the governor's side. At the same time there were also external forces that were drawing the merchants and the office holders together. Historian Murray Greenwood has described the development of a "garrison mentality" among certain English-speaking leaders. In the immediate aftermath of the French Revolution these men believed that France might support an uprising of the French population of Lower Canada in which "the English [would be] marked out as the first victims."[3]

---

3. F. Murray Greenwood, "The Development of a Garrison Mentality Among the English in Lower Canada, 1793-1811", Ph.D. Thesis, University of British Columbia, 1970, p. 21.

Thus forged by both internal and external circumstances, by the early 1800s this alliance, largely made up of English-speaking merchants and officials who were defenders of the power of the governor, formed a coherent political force. In the years leading up to 1837 they were known under various names: the British Party, the Château Clique, the Merchants' Party, and the Bureaucratic Party. Consistently, this political movement was disproportionately made up of English speakers who defended the governor against the assembly.

All English speakers did not, however, belong to the British Party. After all, the Constitutional Act of 1791 did more than establish a new form of government; it also set the stage for the massive influx into the Eastern Townships and the Ottawa Valley of American immigrants. The arrival of these people in the colony significantly altered the place of English speakers within Lower Canadian politics. The newcomers had nothing that bound them to the governor and their experience in the United States, in some cases on the American side in the revolution, gave them a certain favourable disposition towards the assembly's demands for greater power.

Strangely, neither the governor's friends nor the French leaders in the assembly seemed to understand that these new English speakers came to Quebec with ideas different from those of the British Party. Accordingly, Governor Craig was encouraged to facilitate this movement from the South by Chief Justice Jonathan Sewell, who simplistically explained that the "newcomers were of 'English stock, professing the same religion [and] speaking the same language.'"[4] As for the Parti Canadien, the major force in the assembly against the governor's rule, its newspaper *Le Canadien*

---

4. Mason Wade, *The French Canadians* (Toronto, 1968), p. 117.

described the Americans as "a half-savage people whose forays are as much to be feared in Canada as those made formerly by the Goths and Vandals into Italy."[5]

Fearful that the arrival of these new English speakers might eventually swamp the French majority, the assembly did little through the first two decades of the nineteenth century to facilitate their progress. Roads were not built, electoral districts for the Eastern Townships were not established, nor was a judicial district formed for the area. When the British Party led a drive in 1822 to re-unite the Canadas, there was a certain support from the Townships, some of whose residents had come to the conclusion that the elimination of the French-controlled assembly of Lower Canada was essential. In one petition to the British authorities, a group of Townshippers saw this union "as the only effectual means of terminating the difficulties and troubles under which [we] have laboured in times past."[6] But in spite of petitions of this sort there were also Townshippers who were deeply bothered by the heavy handed nature of the union plan and its overt aim of undermining a representative institution. As Fernand Ouellet has noted, "Many in Lower Canada disliked the secrecy of its preparation, its punitive nature, and, for a variety of reasons, its objectives."[7]

The Union Bill of 1822 provided an issue over which the English-speaking population of Lower Canada was divided. However, the English-speaking opposition came not only from the American element within the linguistic minority. The continued existence of the Lower Canadian assembly was also supported by certain people who had come directly from Britain

---

5. *Ibid.*

6. Adam Shortt and Arthur Doughty, *Documents Relating to the Constitutional History of Canada* (Ottawa, 1935), III, p. 131.

7. Ouellet, *Lower Canada*, p. 257.

and whose numbers had been growing since the end of the Napoleonic Wars in 1815. The most prominent of these British immigrants arrived in Quebec, however, in 1790. John Neilson came to Quebec from Scotland to serve as an apprentice at the *Quebec Gazette*, which had been founded by his uncle and inherited by his brother. Neilson became its editor and proprietor in 1796. He was first elected to the assembly in 1818, and quickly moved to the side of the leader of the Parti Canadien, Louis-Joseph Papineau, when the Union Bill was announced. As Neilson noted: "'This is a case of the only lamb of the poor man, which is seized by the rich man to add to the luxury of his feast.'"[8]

The Neilson-Papineau team defeated the Union Bill, and throughout the 1820s the two men worked together to advance the interests of the assembly. This body did not always respond to the concerns of English-speaking merchants, but was far from indifferent to the concerns of less powerful English Quebecers. In order to respond to the "colonists of American origin who were more alert to democratic ideas", a variety of initiatives were taken by the assembly to ease the lot of Townshippers. Roads were built, a judicial district was established, and increased political representation was granted.[9] There is even evidence to indicate that this spirit of co-operation bore fruit for the Parti Canadien for it extended its political base into English-speaking regions of the colony. Within the English-speaking population support for Neilson's views grew to the point that the English Party was all but removed from the assembly in the election of 1827.[10]

8. Wade, pp. 131-132.
9. Ouellet, *Economic and Social History*, p. 366.
10. Ouellet, Lower Canada, p. 259.

One must remember, however, that the English Party did not depend upon the assembly for its power. Rather, it depended upon the governor, and throughout the 1820s the conflicts between the governor and the assembly escalated to the point that massive petitions were sent to London in 1828 to support the assembly's position. One petition with 87,000 signatures and marks emanated from the French-speaking population, while a second with 10,000 names came from the Townships. In response, a commission of inquiry was established by the British House of Commons, and its report conceded many of the Papineau-Neilson demands, most notably a greater control by the assembly over funds for the civil service. While Neilson was generally satisfied with the report, Papineau rejected it because it failed to give clear ascendancy to the assembly. As a result the Papineau-Neilson partnership dissolved, and English Quebec was cut adrift from the major political shift of the 1830s, the movement from protest to rebellion. In a sort of farewell letter to his ex-ally, Papineau wrote to Neilson, "You are disposed to believe that the government can be pushed into the right path and that it will follow it passably well; I am disposed to believe it goes from bad to worse." [11]

Throughout the 1830s Papineau and his allies moved to confront the governor on the very issue of his right to rule. In 1834 the 92 resolutions were steered through the assembly by Papineau to give the clear message that independence might even be considered if the demands of the Patriotes were ignored. Having played their cards, Papineau and his colleagues stumbled into a rebellion in 1837, but they did it with little support or sympathy from the English population.

---

11. Wade, p. 138.

John Neilson
(Helen Taft Manning,
*The Revolt of French Canada,
1800-35*)

Robert Nelson
(Public Archives of Canada,
C-26836)

This is not to say that no English speakers were sympathetic to the rebels' cause. In fact, some of Papineau's leading lieutenants were English speakers. There were the Nelson brothers, Wolfred and Robert, the Irish newspaperman E.B. O'Callaghan, and the merchant T.S. Brown. Robert Nelson was sufficiently important in the Patriote movement that he led the 1838 "invasion" of Quebec attempted by some of the Patriotes who had fled the country during the skirmishes of 1837.

There were also the Irish, some of whom continued to vote for Parti Patriote candidates after all other English-speakers had been scared off.[12] The Irish also provided physical support in the battle of St-Eustache in 1837. Having arrived in large numbers for the first time in the early 1830s, the Irish were not welcomed by certain Patriote leaders who saw them as part of a plot by the British authorities against the French. When the immigrants of 1832 brought cholera with them, one Patriote responded as follows: "It was not enough [for the British] to send among us avaricious egotists... to enrich themselves at the expense of the Canadians and then to enslave them; they must also rid themselves of their beggars and cast them by thousands on our shores; they must send us miserable beings, who, after having partaken of the bread of our children, will subject them to the horrors following upon hunger and misery; they must do still more, they must send us in their train pestilence and death."[13] In spite of such statements the Irish still had cause to adhere to the Patriote position. Situated at the bottom of Quebec's occupational structure, the Irish had little to lose by supporting the rebel cause, and they had their own tradition of scorn for British rule to fuel their sympathy for Papineau.

---

12. France Galarneau, "L'élection partielle du quartier-ouest de Montréal en 1832: analyse politico-sociale", *Revue d'histoire de l'Amérique française*, XXXII (1979), 565-584.

13. Wade, p. 142.

In spite of these indications of isolated English-speaking support for the Patriotes, they should not be overemphasized. In his list of 21,000 Patriotes, historian Jean-Paul Bernard was able to find less than 8 % whose names indicated that they were English-speaking at a time when roughly 25 % of the Lower Canadian population was English-speaking. As a result, Bernard found it impossible to deny "le caractère significatif du clivage anglophones/francophones" in the events of the 1830s.[14] This was one of those rare moments when a certain political unanimity existed within the English-speaking population.

Although they had decided not to support the Patriotes, there were still various political options open to the English speakers in the 1830s. The range of alternatives that existed was expressed in the meetings of the numerous Constitutional Associations that were formed between 1834 and 1837. These associations held rallies across Lower Canada, including the "Great Loyal Meetings" of 1837 which were attended by 7000 people in both Montreal and Quebec City. To be sure, there were many English speakers within these associations who subscribed to the old ideas of the British Party. Nothing would have pleased them more than to crush the Patriotes and revitalize the role of the governor. There were also, however, people such as John Neilson who subscribed to an alternative somewhere between the extremes of the Patriotes and the British Party. Neilson hoped for the preservation of French political power via the assembly along with the continuation of a limited role for the governor.[15] Accordingly, while some English speakers cheered the failure of the rebellions as an opportunity to finish the work of the Conquest, others such as John Neilson hoped that the post-1837 era might see the creation of a

14. Bernard, p. 323.
15. Philip Goldring, "British Colonists and Imperial Interests in Lower Canada, 1830-41", D.Phil., University of London, 1978.

political system in which English and French-speaking Quebecers might be able to work together.

3. 1838-1864

The years immediately following the rebellions provided more cause for celebration among the successors to the camp followers than they did for the more conciliatory followers of John Neilson. Beginning in 1838 Lower Canada was ruled by a special council whose members were generally sympathetic to the merchants' point of view. The work of the special council came to an end in 1841 with the introduction of the union of the Canadas. In design, this union had a striking similarity to the one which had been proposed in 1822. Following upon the recommendations of Lord Durham, Upper and Lower Canada were to be united so as to submerge the French Canadians under an English-speaking majority. During his short stay in the colony to look into the causes of the rebellions, Durham had found "two nations warring in the bosom of a single state", and the union was designed to give a dominant position to the English-speaking "nation" at the expense of the other. Durham wanted to see the united Canadas ruled by an elected assembly which would hold most of the power, while the governor would control very little.[16] He felt comfortable with such a recommendation because the union offered the promise of a predominantly English-speaking assembly. Not all of Durham's recommendations were heeded, however, so that when the union came into force in 1841 it was with a government structure almost identical to that which had existed prior to 1837. The powers of the elected assembly were still limited by the executive and legislative councils whose members were still to be appointed by the governor.

16. Gerald Craig, ed., *Lord Durham's Report* (Toronto, 1963).

This structure was perfectly suited to the leading business interests of Quebec's English-speaking minority. As long as the councils remained under the control of the governor, they had cause to hope that English speakers sympathetic to their point of view might be disproportionately represented. Indeed, when the governor's power to select the members of the executive council ended in 1848 three of Quebec's five posts were held by English speakers. Similarly, prior to the conversion of the legislative council into an elected body in 1856, English-speaking businessmen from Quebec were strongly represented.[17]

Even within the assembly there was reason for the merchants to be pleased at the start of the 1840s. Not only had an English majority been created by the union, but among English-speaking voters in Quebec there was a tendency to support candidates sympathetic to the merchants as opposed to those allied with John Neilson. Neilson campaigned against the implementation of the union in the elections of 1841. He felt that it was a punitive action against the French-speaking majority of Lower Canada, a position that he had also held in 1822; but while some English-speaking Quebecers rallied to his side in the 1820s such was not the case following the bitterness of the rebellions. In the French parts of Quebec the elections of 1841 saw battles between candidates for and against the union. By contrast, in numerous English-speaking ridings both of the candidates were pro-union reflecting the limited support for Neilson's views.[18]

Throughout the 1840s Neilson, along with most French-speaking members of the assembly, complained about both the weak position of the French

---

17. André Garon, "Le conseil législatif au Canada-Uni", *Social History,* VIII (1971), pp. 61-83.
18. Paul Cornell, *The Alignment of Political Groups in Canada, 1841-67* (Toronto, 1962), p. 5.

population within the union and the arbitrary power still held by the governor. By the time of Neilson's death in 1848, however, both of these concerns had been resolved to a certain degree. French political power was resurrected through an alliance within the assembly of certain moderate elements from each side of the Ottawa River. The resulting Lafontaine-Baldwin partnership had as its goal the achievement of responsible government, that is, the control over the executive council by the assembly. Britain accepted this principle in 1847, and when the Lafontaine-Baldwin team won the election of 1847-8 it chose the members of the new executive council (cabinet), leaving the governor with little more than a symbolic role to play.

The governor's loss of ability to influence events meant the death of the British Party, a fixture of English- Quebec politics since the Conquest. After all, what point was there in supporting the governor when Britain no longer supported him? English speakers had one last opportunity to show their dismay over this new state of affairs in early 1849. When the assembly passed a bill to provide compensation for losses in Lower Canada incurred during the Rebellion of 1837, the loyal supporters of the British Party looked to the governor, Lord Elgin, to reject what they saw as compensation to the rebels. Elgin had no choice but to adhere to the wishes of the assembly; this was the essence of responsible government. In protest, however, English speakers took part in the stoning of the governor and, more dramatically, the burning of the parliament building which was then located in Montreal. A sequel to these acts of despair took place later in the year when members of Montreal's business elite affixed their names to a manifesto calling for the union of Canada and the United States.[19]

---

19. J.M.S. Careless, *The Union of the Canadas* (Toronto, 1967), pp. 122-131.

By the mid-1850s these passions had long since passed, and the political struggles within Canada East no longer pertained to the structure of the government but rather to the policies to be pursued. By the middle of the decade, two political parties had emerged, both of which would persist into the post-Confederation period. The more conservative of the two was the Bleu party headed by George-Etienne Cartier. The Bleus stood for the defense of business interests. This party was therefore a logical vehicle for the leading English-speaking businessmen in the colony once they had recovered from the introduction of responsible government. Other English speakers, who followed more in the tradition of John Neilson, allied themselves with the Rouges who were vocal supporters of French-speaking interests and frequent opponents of business demands. Influential politicians such as Luther Holton, Christopher Dunkin and L.S. Huntingdon were sympathetic to the Rouges. As historian Paul Cornell has noted, both parties consistently had "an English element in [their] ranks."[20] In fact, in the elections held between 1857 and 1863 there was scarcely any difference between the political affiliations of deputies elected in English-speaking ridings and those chosen in French ridings.[21]

As Confederation approached, there was no sign of the political unanimity that had existed among English-speaking Quebecers in the years leading up to and following the rebellions. Rather, English speakers were divided on the issues of the day much as the French-speaking majority was divided. Consequently,

---

20. Cornell, p. 84.
21. This assertion is based upon an analysis of the victorious party in each riding in each election between 1857 and 1863. English ridings, defined as those where a majority of the population was English-speaking, returned *Bleu* candidates in 75 % of the cases. The remaining ridings returned the Bleus only slightly less frequently, 66 % of the time.

a real debate took place within the English-speaking population when the Confederation issue took hold beginning in 1864.

4. 1864-1867

The debate within the English-speaking population regarding Confederation once again provides a perfect opportunity to examine the various divisions within that minority. By 1864 a variety of issues had converged to make Confederation a serious possibility. Politically, the Union of the Canadas was no longer working, given the coalitions that had emerged. A new coalition had to be forged to get around this impasse, and in 1864 it was formed on the basis of support for a confederation of the various British North American colonies. This movement was facilitated by sympathy from business interests, most notably the Grand Trunk Railway, whose profits stood to increase with the achievement of Confederation. In addition, the American Civil War massed a large army on the doorstep of British North America, creating a fear (undoubtedly manipulated by pro-Confederation sympathizers) that when the war was over the North might conquer the British colonies if unity were not achieved. At the same time, Britain, which had been embarrassed by the South's use of British North American ports, was eager to see the creation of a new nation so as to extricate itself from such situations.

Thus the stage was set for a Canadian delegation to attend a meeting of Maritimers being held in September 1864 to discuss Maritime union. Before that meeting was over, agreement in principle had been reached regarding a wider union, and the delegates decided to reassemble in Quebec City in October. Out of these later meetings came the Quebec Resolutions which formed a rough draft for the British North

America Act. It was on the basis of these resolutions that the legislature of the still united Canadas debated the virtues of Confederation in 1865. This was as close to a vote on Confederation as would ever take place, since John A. Macdonald had firmly instructed the leaders of the colonies not to take the issue to the people if at all possible. In New Brunswick, however, the mandate of the government had expired, and in the election of 1865 the pro-Confederation forces were defeated, thus confirming Macdonald's fears.

The Quebec Resolutions contained many, but not all, of the provisions of interest to English-speaking Quebecers that ultimately appeared in the BNA Act. What were complete, however, were those provisions that related to business concerns. This should come as little surprise given the prominent role of English-speaking business interests, particularly those concentrated in Montreal, in pushing for Confederation. The Quebec Resolutions set out the basic division of powers between the federal and provincial governments, with the former exercising control in those fields important to men interested in solidifying their dominance over a trans-continental economy. Banks were to be controlled by Ottawa so that the leaders of institutions such as the Bank of Montreal might easily extend their influence across provincial borders; and railways that crossed such boundaries were to fall under federal jurisdiction so that Montreal might emerge as the transportation centre of the new nation. By the 1860s Montreal had eclipsed Quebec City as a business center, while Toronto was not yet a serious rival. The BNA Act was written, in certain regards, by and for the city's English-speaking business elite.

The Quebec Resolutions also responded to certain fears that the English-speaking population had about its place within the soon-to-be-created province of Quebec. Had Macdonald had his way there would have been no provincial governments, but he knew that French-speaking Quebecers would never have gone along with a legislative union. But if there was going to be a Quebec government with jurisdiction over certain specified areas, it would only be with some explicit guarantees for the English-speaking minority. Accordingly, leaders such as Alexander Galt sought to prevent the transaction in French only of business in the Quebec legislature by the inclusion of Article 46 in the Quebec Resolutions. This provision later surfaced in the BNA Act as Article 133. It stipulated that both French and English were to be used in the courts and legislature of Quebec. The French-speaking minorities in the other original provinces were powerless to secure such a provision.

The clout of certain English-speaking Quebecers was also evident in the Quebec Resolutions in terms of the provisions relating to education. The provinces were to have complete control over education except when it came to "the rights and privileges which the Protestant or Catholic minority in both Canadas [might] possess as to their denominational schools at the time when the Union [went] into operation."[22] Given the relative influence of Protestants in Lower Canada and of Catholics in Upper Canada, it is obvious that this clause was inserted in the interest of the former group. Similarly, the Quebec Resolutions catered to the concerns of certain English-speaking Quebecers in the manner in which representatives were to be appointed to the Senate. Quebec's senators were to be designated as representing specific ridings so as to assure the appointment of English-speaking representatives from regions such as the Eastern Townships and the Ottawa Valley. Needless to say, no comparable treatment was accorded to linguistic minorities in the other provinces.

22. *Quebec Resolutions*, Article 43.1; *BNA ACT*, Article 93.2.

But as generous as these provisions might appear they did not result in unanimous support from the English-speaking Quebecers who debated the resolutions in the legislature of the united Canadas in 1865. To be sure, there were Montreal business leaders, such as John Rose, who were convinced that this was a good deal for Quebec's linguistic minority. He asserted in the debates: "The English-speaking minority in Lower Canada has considered the resolutions carefully, and with all their prejudices versus it at the outset, are now warmly in its favour."[23] Alexander Galt, by contrast, was more guarded in his support. Galt's business connections prevented him from opposing the resolutions, but his identity as a Townshipper made him sufficiently insecure to fight for more. In regard to education, for instance, Galt wanted greater rights for the Protestant minority prior to the date of the union so as to get more out of the educational guarantees noted above.

There were also those who truly followed in Neilson's footsteps, who had some sympathies for the Rouges, and who saw the resolutions as hostile to French-speaking interests. For those English speakers, there was no question of voting "yes" in 1865. In a perceptive linking of French rights in Canada and English rights in Quebec, Christopher Dunkin challenged the views of the business elite: "The French will find themselves a minority in the General [federal] legislature... They will thus be compelled to be aggressive to secure and retain their power. There will be in this system the very strongest tendencies to make the French aggressive upon the rights of the minority [in Quebec], and at the same time to make the minority suspicious."[24] Four other English Quebecers sided with

---

23. P.B. Waite, ed., *The Confederation Debates in the Province of Canada* (Toronto, 1963), p. 101.
24. *Ibid.*, pp. 119-120.

Dunkin, and while not insignificant these men were decidedly in the minority, as the other eleven English members voted "yes". Among the French-speaking deputies the vote was somewhat closer, with 27 in favour of the resolutions and 21 against. As to what the general population thought, it will never be known.

In the two years between this debate and the implementation of the BNA Act, Galt and his colleagues tried to sweeten the pot for the English minority, perhaps in recognition of the constituency that Dunkin represented. As we saw in the previous chapter, Galt was unable to steer the Langevin Bill through the legislature so as to broaden the powers of the Protestants when it came to educational matters. While Galt did succeed in gaining an expanded role for the federal government should the rights of a religious minority be violated, his failure to broaden the nature of those rights led to his resignation from the government prior to 1 July 1867. By contrast, he was more successful in securing inclusion of Article 80, also discussed in Chapter IV, by which the boundaries of certain provincial ridings were to be immune from change. Similarly, he contributed to the drafting of articles, between 1865 and 1867, to make Quebec the only province with an upper house. The basis for appointments to the legislative council was to be the same as that noted earlier with regard to Quebec's representatives to the Senate. English-speaking Quebecers were to be over-represented in the legislative council to block any anti-English legislation coming from the assembly.

In its final form the BNA Act provides a guide to the various forces within the English-speaking population of Quebec. Leading the way were Montreal business leaders who were about to enter into a half century of unprecedented power. These men were

Alexander Galt
(Public Archives of
Canada, PA-13008)

Thomas D'Arcy McGee
(Public Archives
of Canada,
C-51976)

interested in the concentration of economic decision-making at the federal level. On the provincial level they joined with other Protestants to secure the guarantees for denominational education in Article 93. No guarantees were to be included, however, for the English-speaking Catholics, whose fate was left in the hands of the Catholic hierarchy. The leading Irish politician from Quebec at the time, D'Arcy McGee, was an unqualified supporter of Confederation, but his Irish support dried up in his election to Parliament in 1867. At least one commentator has noted that this had some connection with McGee's failure to secure educational guarantees for the English-Catholic population.[25] Finally, there were the regional concerns that were addressed by Article 80 and by the provisions relevant to the system of representation for both the Senate and the legislative council. If one knew nothing else about the composition of the English- speaking population of Quebec on 1 July 1867, the BNA Act would provide a host of clues.

5. Conclusion

There were only a few moments in the century leading up to Confederation during which English-speaking Quebecers were of one mind concerning political issues. The most conspicuous of these English speakers were the business leaders who were prepared to do what was necessary to advance their interests. In the 1760s this led them to contest the power of the governor, who was to become their patron by the early 1800s. By the 1860s their business interests led them to push for Confederation. However, while these businessmen may have been the most powerful English

---

25. Nolte, "The Irish in Canada".

Quebecers, they were rarely in a position to speak for the entire population. Between 1760 and 1791 the camp followers had to deal with opponents such as Adam Mabane, while in the years leading up to 1837 their views were contested by such diverse groups as the Americans who had come to settle in the Eastern Townships and the Irish. The British Party also had to confront men such as John Neilson who were ideologically opposed to any weakening of the political institutions of Lower Canada. In the years leading up to Confederation men such as John Rose, Alexander Galt, D'Arcy McGee and Christopher Dunkin continued to speak for the specific segments of the English-speaking population that they represented. These various political figures provided a reflection of the diverse elements that made up the pre-Confederation English-speaking population.

SELECT BIBLIOGRAPHY

Burt, A.L. *The Old Province of Quebec.* Toronto, 1933.

Cornell, Paul. *The Alignment of Political Groups in Canada, 1841-1867.* Toronto, 1962.

Neatby, Hilda. *Quebec: The Revolutionary Age.* Toronto, 1966.

Ouellet, Fernand. *Lower Canada, 1791-1840: Social Change and Nationalism.* Toronto, 1980.

Waite, P.B., ed. *The Confederation Debates in the Province of Canada.* Toronto, 1963.

Part II

Confederation to Referendum, 1867-1980

English-speaking Quebecers were fortunate that Confederation occurred when it did. The concessions that they secured in the BNA Act reflected certain aspects of the strength of the population at the time. In 1867 English speakers, for all their divisions, were united by ties with Britain, were prominent in various regions of the province, and made up nearly one-quarter of Quebec's population. Moreover, the English-speaking business leaders were among the most powerful in North America. By contrast, by the time of the 1980 referendum on sovereignty-association nearly all of these characteristics had been altered. The English speakers of 1980 were no longer united by ethnic ties, and they were heavily concentrated only in Montreal. They represented just 11 % of the total Quebec population, and even their business leaders had fallen on hard times. These various changes took place gradually during the post-Confederation period, and as a result English-speaking Quebecers wielded considerably less political power after 1867 than before.

VI

The Changing Ethnic Composition of English-Speaking Quebec

English speakers constituted an ever-growing percentage of the Quebec population throughout most of the pre-Confederation era because of the large scale arrival of English-speaking immigrants. It was essential for the growth of the English-speaking population that these newcomers arrive in large numbers because many would soon move on to other parts of North America. This substantial influx of immigrants counterbalanced the birth rate among French speakers which was consistently higher than that for English-speaking Quebecers. Successive waves of immigrants permitted the English-speaking population to make up 25 % of the Quebec total by the mid-1800s. First the Americans arrived, and after the War of 1812 immigrants came from various parts of Britain. In addition to contributing to the expansion of the English-speaking population, these immigrants also provided a certain cohesiveness within the minority as most of them came to Quebec with the ability to trace their roots back to Britain.

In the post-Confederation period the tendency for English speakers to move on to other parts of the continent persisted, as did the relatively high birth rate

among French-speaking Quebecers.[1] What changed
after 1867, however, were both the extent and the
composition of the immigrant population that arrived
to form part of the linguistic minority. When the large
scale migrations to Quebec from Britain fell off in the
1850s there was no new group to fill the void. One
observer has noted that during the quarter-century
from 1844 to 1879 "Canada received only a few more
British immigrants than during the ten year period
1845 to 1854"; nor did this situation greatly change
until after the turn of the century.[2] As a result, the
absolute size of the English-speaking population increased only modestly between 1871 and 1901 while
the relative place of English speakers within the Quebec population declined from 20 % to 17 %.

In the twentieth century the percentage of Quebecers with English as their mother tongue continued
to decline, reaching 11 % by 1981. Until the decade of
the 1970s this decline was only a relative one, for the
resumption of large-scale immigration to Quebec resulted in the absolute growth of the population. For
instance, while the English-speaking population grew
by only 19 % between 1871 and 1901, there was a 50 %
increase during the following three decades. The 20 %
increase in the single decade of the 1920s was cut to
9 % in the 1930s owing to the freeze on immigration
caused first by the depression and then by World War
II. However, with the end of the war the 20 % figure
was reached again in the 1940s and 1950s. Under the
pressure of the stepped-up movement of English
speakers to other provinces in the 1960s there was only
a 13 % increase during that decade; and when the
losses to other provinces were combined with a falling
off of immigration there was a 10 % decline in the

---

1. Gary Caldwell, *A Demographic Profile of the English-Speaking Population
   of Quebec, 1921-71* (Quebec, 1974), p. 41.
2. Lloyd Reynolds, *The British Immigrant* (Toronto, 1935), pp. 33-34.

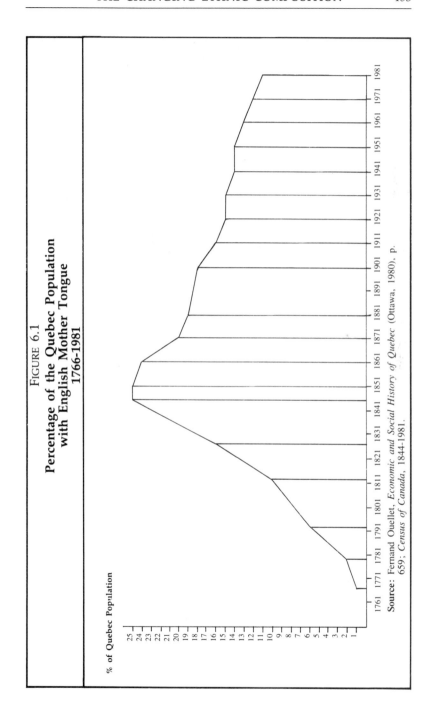

FIGURE 6.1
Percentage of the Quebec Population
with English Mother Tongue
1766-1981

% of Quebec Population

Source: Fernand Ouellet, *Economic and Social History of Quebec* (Ottawa, 1980). p. 659; *Census of Canada*, 1844-1981.

1970s. This decline was of roughly the same dimensions as that experienced in the 1860s and had at its roots the same two factors: a decline in the number of newcomers arriving from abroad and an increase in the movement of resident English speakers to other parts of North America.

While these factors were influential in determining the rate of growth of the English-speaking population, they also were responsible for profound changes in the ethnic composition of this population during the post-Confederation period. In 1871 the English-speaking population was almost exclusively of British origin, and within that British population the Irish made up the single largest group. In the century that followed, however, the large scale departure of many Irish Quebecers from the province together with considerable immigration from England allowed the English to dominate. A further change in the ethnic composition of the English-speaking population occurred between 1931 and 1981. When mother tongue information was first reported in the 1931 census, only 5% of the English mother tongue population was not of British origin. This figure grew to 40% by 1981 as a result of considerable immigration from Europe and the massive departure of Quebecers of British origin in the 1970s. The changes that are evident from the tables below indicate just how profoundly English-speaking Quebec was transformed in the post-Confederation era. In the sections that follow, the transformation of the British origin population and the emergence of the non-British element will be examined.

TABLE 6.1

Ethnic Composition
of Quebec's British Origin Population,
1871-1981

	IRISH		SCOTTISH		ENGLISH	
	Number	% British Origin Population	Number	% British Origin Population	Number	% British Origin Population
1871	123,478	51	49,458	20	69,822	29
1881	123,749	47	54,923	21	81,513	32
1901	114,842	39	60,068	21	114,710	40
1911	103,147	32	58,555	18	153,295	48
1921	94,947	27	63,915	18	196,982	55
1931	108,312	25	87,300	20	234,739	54
1941	109,894	24	90,582	20	249,548	55
1951	110,189	22	89,620	18	289,045	59
1961	129,326	22	109,937	19	322,410	57
1981	97,860	21	62,500	14	295,485	64

Source: *Census of Canada.*

1. The British Element

In the half century following Confederation the British origin population of Quebec was transformed as the Irish and English groups exchanged places. In 1871, 51 % of all British origin Quebecers could trace their roots back to Ireland while 29 % had ties with England; by 1921 the Irish figure had been reduced to 27 % while the English share had grown to 55 %. This transformation was partly the result of a precipitous decline in the absolute number of Irish Quebecers. Between 1871 and 1921 the ranks of the Irish were reduced by nearly one quarter, largely because of the drying up of Irish immigration to Quebec and the substantial movement of the resident Irish to other

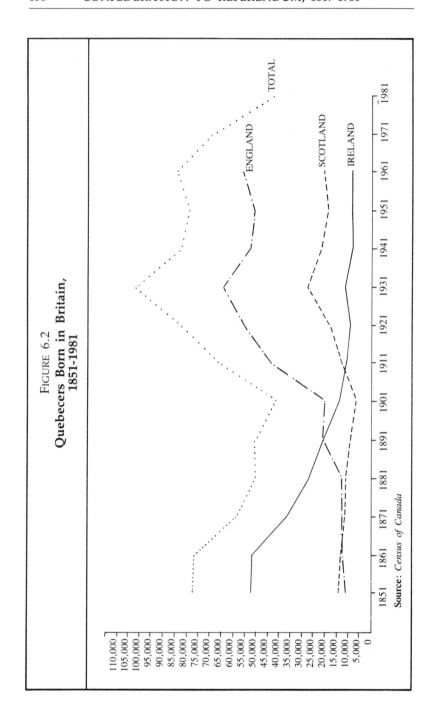

FIGURE 6.2
Quebecers Born in Britain,
1851-1981

Source: *Census of Canada*

parts of North America. The decline of Irish immigration is evident in Figure 6.2 which depicts the steady
erosion of the Irish-born population of Quebec in the
absence of any new blood to bolster its ranks.

As for the movement from Quebec of the Irish
who were already settled there, this was a process
which had begun in the pre-Confederation period and
which was linked to the marginal place of the Irish in
the Quebec economy. There was a significant drop in
the number of Irish-born Quebecers between 1861 and
1871, many of whom undoubtedly left the Quebec City
area in the wake of the demise of the timber trade. The
continued departure of the Irish into the post-1867
period was evident from the drastic reduction in their
numbers outside Montreal between 1871 and 1941.
None of the three British groups noted in Table 6.2
benefited from immigration to bolster their ranks outside Montreal in the post-Confederation period. The
more pronounced decline in the Irish population was a
clear reflection of the greater inclination of the Irish to
leave these outlying parts of the province.[3]

TABLE 6.2
Changes in the British Origin Population, 1871-1941

Percentage Change Between 1871 and 1941

	IRISH	SCOTTISH	ENGLISH
Montreal Region	+92 %	+361 %	+912 %
Rest of Quebec	−48 %	− 14 %	+ 54 %

Source: *Census of Canada.*

---

3. It would seem that the Irish remained the poorest of the three British
groups in rural Quebec well into the twentieth century, a situation
no doubt linked to their departure from rural areas of the province.
See, for instance, Clarke McIntosh, "Devolution and Survival of the
Rural English-Speaking Population in the Region North of Quebec
City", B.A. Thesis, McGill University, 1976.

What happened to the Irish who departed from rural Quebec is not entirely clear. Some went to Montreal, thus contributing to the growth of the Irish population in the city between 1871 and 1941. This growth was insignificant, however, compared to that experienced by the English and Scottish groups in Montreal, which benefited from the arrival of a significant number of immigrants early in the twentieth century. Those Irish who did not go to Montreal probably left the province altogether. Indeed, Gary Caldwell has noted that for English speakers in general "the great majority who [left] non-metropolitan Quebec [moved] outside the province rather than to Montreal."[4]

A further possible explanation as to what happened to the Irish Quebecers outside Montreal is related to the census definition of ethnicity. Since ethnicity was defined through the father's family, any marriage between members of different ethnic groups threatened the continuation, as far as the census was concerned, of one of the two groups into the next generation. As the Irish population outside Montreal shrank, it became increasingly difficult for the remaining Irish to marry within their own group, and since they were the most Catholic of the three British origin groups they frequently selected French-Catholic mates. When an Irish woman married a French man, the offspring were counted by the census taker as being of French origin, the Irish links thus becoming invisible to the historian. However, there is another way to show that such marriages were more common among the Irish than among the Scots or the English. When an Irish man married a French woman, the children were considered of Irish origin although there was a considerable likelihood that they would have French as their mother tongue. Accordingly, in 1941 11 % of all

---

4. Caldwell, pp. 61-63.

Irish Quebecers claimed French as their mother tongue, roughly twice the rate for other British origin residents of the province.

The experience of the English origin population in the post-confederation period stands in stark contrast to that of the Irish. This group rarely had members whose mother tongue was French and was less likely to see its members depart from rural Quebec. Most significantly, however, the English origin population was nourished by the substantial immigration that began roughly at the turn of the century. The number of Quebecers born in England hovered around 12,000 from 1851 to 1881. Then, in the 1880s there was a significant increase in the number of English-born, which tailed off in the 1890s. Beginning in the first decade of the new century, however, there was a spectacular increase in both the English and the Scottish-born populations. Between 1901 and 1931 the number of Quebecers born in these two lands increased from roughly 28,000 to over 90,000, in the process nearly doubling the population of Quebec that was of either English or Scottish origin.

Most of these immigrants settled in Montreal, thus contributing to the steady concentration of the English-speaking population in the metropolis. Many came to Montreal to occupy certain specific positions in the Quebec economy, and in so doing they also contributed to a transformation of the place of English speakers within the economy. While the Irish left Quebec, in part, because of their marginal position in the economy, the new British immigrants of the early twentieth century arrived to take advantage of skilled jobs that were just becoming available. These jobs were particularly concentrated in the metal trades. Some positions were to be found in the ever-expanding shops of the Grand Trunk Railway. One such position was filled by the grandfather of historian Terry Copp. As Copp has

English Immigrants at Quebec City, 1911 (Public Archives of Canada, PA-10494)

Canadian Pacific Railway's Montreal Shops (Public Archives of Canada, PA-24510)

noted, "My maternal grandfather was recruited by the Grand Trunk Railway in 1905. He left England with a wife and four young children and settled in Verdun."[5]

Still other posts were created in new factories established throughout the city. In Lachine, Dominion Bridge set up shop shortly after the turn of the century, while in the east end an English-speaking population emerged to take advantage of the work available in shops opened in the pre-war years of the new century. There were the Angus shops of the CPR as well as the Montreal Locomotive Works, the Canadian Steel Foundries and the Canadian Vickers shipyards, to name only a few. Lloyd Reynolds has noted that these various firms "brought almost an entire staff of supervisors and skilled workmen from Britain... There was a great demand for artisans, boilermakers, machinists, blacksmiths and numbers of other skilled trades. Britain was the home of the new technology, and British mechanics accordingly found a ready welcome among Canadian employers. English and Scottish artisans dominated the immigration flow as Irish labourers had done at an earlier date."[6] While people of British origin made up only 17 % of Quebec's male labour force in 1931, this figure reached 28 % for those in the metal trades.

These British immigrants also moved into new jobs that were opening up in the tertiary sector. In particular, jobs were being created in the offices of large firms based in Montreal whose operations extended beyond the borders of Quebec. For institutions such as banks and insurance companies, the need to both read and write in English was essential, thus frequently locking out French-speaking candidates. As a result, in 1931 44 % of all clerical workers in Quebec

---

5. Terry Copp, *The Anatomy of Poverty* (Toronto, 1974), p. 12.
6. Reynolds, pp. 93, 121.

were of British origin as opposed to 17 % of the total workforce. A similar over-representation was evident among the British born who occupied 12 % of all clerical jobs, nearly twice their share of the provincial workforce. Lloyd Reynolds found evidence of these clerical workers in the Montreal neighbourhood of Notre Dame de Grâce (N.D.G.), which he described in 1935 as "a predominantly clerical area lying to the west of Westmount. Composed largely of open fields in 1921, today [it] contains some 50,000 persons." The area attracted "not merely new immigrants arriving since [the first world] war, but also those who [were] economically successful in one of the older immigrant areas and who wish[ed] to register their economic success through a change of residence." N.D.G. also was home for the children of British immigrants whose parents had worked in factories but who had now "graduated to the clerical class."[7]

The flow of English and Scottish immigrants to Quebec was checked in the 1930s, first by the depression and later by World War II. Following the war this source of English speakers never returned to the high level of the early years of the century. In the 1950s, for instance, there was only a 6 % increase in the number of British-born in Quebec, a far cry from the 60 % increase recorded in the period between 1901 and 1911. Moreover, this was a very small increase in a period of substantial immigration from other parts of Europe to Quebec. In the 1960s and 1970s the number of British-born Quebecers was cut in half, although the available information does not make it possible to separate the various groups within that population.

The significant decline of the 1960s and 1970s was the product of two phenomena: a slowing down of immigration together with the movement of British

---

7. *Ibid.*, pp. 128-129.

origin Quebecers to other provinces. Between 1956 and 1961 the number of people of British origin who came to Quebec from other provinces was roughly equal to the number that left.[8] By the 1960s, however, English-speaking Quebecers were leaving Quebec for other provinces faster than they could be replaced, and at the same time the British-born population was in absolute decline. Evidently, some of the British-born already settled in Quebec were leaving, while no newcomers from Britain were arriving to take their places. In the 1970s the exodus from Quebec became so great that the British origin population declined by 17 %, the first such absolute decline since the 1860s. Among those Quebecers who were of British origin and who had English as their mother tongue, the decline was 21 %.

The accelerated departure of English speakers from the province between 1976 and 1981 was undoubtedly linked to political factors. How else can one explain the fact that the net loss of English speakers to other provinces between 1976 and 1981 equalled that experienced between 1966 and 1976? Nevertheless, it is also important to take into account economic factors that had slowed immigration from Britain since World War II and that had contributed to a net loss of English speakers to other provinces by the mid-1960s. Just as the availability of employment in certain sectors of the economy had fuelled the flow of British immigration earlier in the century, now the limited opportunities in such sectors both cut off immigration and encouraged people to leave. It was symbolic, for instance, that the Vickers shipyards, once a source of employment for British immigrants, had closed by 1970. This was reflected by a decline in the number of British origin workers employed in the building of transportation equipment from 7,000 in 1961 to 4,730 ten years later.

8. Caldwell, p. 78.

During the same period the totals for all Quebec workers remained roughly the same. Similarly, while there
was a significant increase between 1931 and 1971 in the
number of Quebec workers in the metal trades, the
British presence declined from over 11,000 in 1931 to
roughly 5,000 four decades later.

Finally, employment prospects in the head offices
of major Montreal firms also dried up in the post-war
era. By the 1960s Toronto had surpassed Montreal in
terms of the number of head offices located within its
boundaries.[9] Those firms that remained catered increasingly to a Quebec market, and as a result a
capacity to function in French became essential, thus
further reducing employment prospects for British origin workers. During the 1970s male employment in the
clerical sector increased by nearly 10 % across Quebec,
but for British origin workers there was an absolute
decline of one-third. For the occupation of bookkeeper,
male employment increased by 30 % across Quebec
between 1971 and 1981, but declined by a comparable
figure among British origin workers.

Throughout the post-Confederation period economic factors played a central role in transforming the
place of the British origin population in Quebec. Economic factors encouraged the departure of that group's
poorest element with the Irish leaving in large numbers. At the same time, job prospects brought English
and Scottish immigrants to take their places. In the
post-war era the British origin population was overwhelmingly English in its composition, but its place
within the English-speaking population declined, partly because economic forces both discouraged further
British immigration and led to the departure of British
origin Quebecers already settled in the province. The
decline in the relative place of people of British origin

---

9. George Nader, *Cities of Canada* (Toronto, 1975), I, 223.

within the English-speaking population was also caused, however, by the growth in the number of English speakers who were of other origins. It is this latter group that will now be discussed.

2. English speakers of Non-British Origins

When the first extensive mother tongue information was presented in the 1931 census, 95 % of all English mother tongue Quebecers were of British origin. The groups that would later play a central role within the English-speaking population were still numerically insignificant. There were, for instance, only 252 Jews who had English as their mother tongue and the figure for Italians was only 725. In spite of these small numbers, Quebec already was home for many members of these two groups by the start of the Great Depression. In 1931 there were 130,000 Quebecers who were of neither French nor British origin, a figure that had grown from only 25,000 in 1881. Jews and Italians accounted for roughly half of the 1931 figure with the Jews forming the single largest group.

The 60,000 Jews living in Quebec in 1931 had come to this side of the Atlantic in the great migrations from central and eastern Europe in the last years of the 1800s and in the first decades of the twentieth century. Like other immigrants who came to Quebec in the post-Confederation period, the Jews settled almost exclusively in Montreal, where they slowly forged ties with the English-speaking population. By the time of the 1931 census, there were few within the Jewish population who claimed English as their mother tongue. Nevertheless, there were nearly 30,000 Jews more than ten years of age who spoke English in addition to their mother tongue, but only 112 who had adopted French as their second language. In the next generation it was unlikely that the old world language would

TABLE 6.3

**Ethnic Composition
of Quebec's English Mother Tongue (EMT) Population,
1931-1981**

	BRITISH		FRENCH		ITALIANS		JEWS		OTHERS	
	Number	% of total EMT population	Number	% of total EMT population	Number	% of total EMT population	Number	% of total EMT population	Number	% of total EMT population
1931	406,833	95	12,653	3	725	—	252	—	9,150	2
1941	413,025	88	25,723	5	1,665	—	10,948	2	17,629	5
1951	449,250	80	45,710	8	3,144	1	28,600	5	31,552	6
1961	511,293	73	68,339	10	6,387	1	40,904	6	70,479	10
1971	528,695	67	88,255	11	14,950	2	73,110	9	83,825	11
1981	417,875	60	102,442	15	18,265	3	57,635	8	98,698	14

Source: *Census of Canada.*

be passed along. English would emerge to take its place, thus adding new members to the English-speaking population. The Jews were rationally responding to the distribution of economic power in Quebec that made English the logical language to pass on to their children.

The depression and then the Second World War brought an end to the massive arrival of European Jews in Quebec. There were other Jewish immigrants in the post-war era, but many of these were French speakers from North Africa who were not candidates for integration into English-speaking Quebec. But in spite of the falling off of European immigration, the natural growth of the Jewish population with English as its mother tongue pushed its numbers to nearly 75,000 by 1971, over 11 % of the total English-speaking population. In the decade of the 1970s, however, the English-speaking population of Jewish origin, like that of British origin, experienced an absolute decline. Both groups saw their numbers reduced by 21 %, as the Jews, like English speakers of British origin, left for both political and economic reasons. The Jews had come to Quebec earlier in the century with little in the way of either capital or skills that could be translated into well-paying positions. Nevertheless, in the post-war era the children and grandchildren of these immigrants moved into various white collar and professional jobs. By 1971, 31 % of all Jewish men were in such positions, a figure twice as large as that for Quebec's male workforce. During the 1970s, when limited economic prospects for English speakers combined with political insecurity, many Jews simply moved on.

While the Jewish and the British elements within the English-speaking population were in decline by the 1970s other groups came to pick up some of the slack. During that decade, for instance, the number of Italians with English as their mother tongue increased by

Temple
Beth Solomon,
Montreal
(Edward Hillel)

Eastern European Immigrants (Public Archives of Canada, PA-127155)

22 %. The Italians, like the Jews, had been settled in Quebec since the beginning of the century, but at the start of the depression the Italian origin population was not even half the size of the Jewish population. Following World War II, however, the relative places of the two groups were reversed as Italians poured into North America in search of jobs. By 1981 there were 163,000 Quebecers of Italian origin while the Jewish total was only 90,000. Other southern European immigrants joined the Italians in the post-war era, and by 1981 there were also roughly 25,000 Quebecers of Portuguese origin and 50,000 who had ties with Greece.

Unlike the Jews the majority of Italians passed French along as the mother tongue of their children as the old language dropped by the wayside. This preference was evident as early as 1931, when there were 725 Italians with English as their mother tongue and 2,422 with French; by 1971 there were 24,445 with French but only 14,950 with English. Had it not been for the precipitous decline of the birthrate among French speakers, the manner in which Italians passed along either English or French to their children would never have become a major issue of controversy. After all, the Jews had overwhelmingly moved into the English-speaking population, while the Italians with their Catholic background had a greater affinity with the French. The Italians' misfortune, however, was that they arrived in large numbers just as the French birth rate was declining. By 1971, of all Quebecers of Italian origin who had either English or French as their mother tongue, 62 % had moved into the French stream. In a province where 81 % of the population had French as its mother tongue, some people were concerned by the fact that a smaller percentage of newcomers were integrating into the French-speaking population. These concerns were believed to be particularly valid in Montreal where one projection envisaged the French population being pushed into a minority situation by the twin forces of a declining French birth rate and a certain integration of the immigrant population into the English stream. [10] In order to try to halt the attraction of English caused by economic factors, Quebec governments introduced Bill 22 in 1974 and Bill 101 in 1977, both of which had as their primary goal the limiting of access to English schools to those who had English as their mother tongue. [11]

These bills had as their long-term goal the routing of Quebec's non-French/non-English population into the French stream. [11] What they could not change, however, was the fact that a significant number of southern European immigrants had already come to have English as their mother tongue. While there was a decline in other English mother tongue groups, the percentage of English speakers who were of Italian origin increased from 3 % in 1971 to 5 % in 1981. Given the fact that Quebecers of French and British origins had lower birthrates than other Quebecers, the Italian share of the English-speaking population was bound to continue to increase as time went on.

The arrival in Quebec during the post-Confederation period of groups such as the Jews and the Italians altered the ethnic homogeneity that had earlier existed. Still other groups arrived to end the racial homogeneity that had long prevailed among English speakers. In the case of Quebec's English-speaking Black population, for instance, the establishment of a real community came only towards the end of the nineteenth century. [12] In the 1860s porters on

10. For one such projection, see Jacques Henripin, "Quebec and the Demographic Dilemma of French Canadian Society", in Dale Thomson, ed., *Quebec Society and Politics: Views from the Inside* (Toronto, 1973), p. 162.
11. Language legislation is further discussed in chapter nine.
12. The census provides no direct evidence of the number of Blacks, let alone English-speaking Blacks, in Quebec. Accordingly, one is forced to use indirect means to gauge the growth of this population.

Pullman cars in the United States were almost exclusively Black, and when service was extended to
Montreal in the 1880s the economic justification for a
Black community in Montreal was established. As historian Robin Winks has noted: "The CP system made
Montreal its general employment centre, while the CN
used the city to hire for its Central and Atlantic divisions. Negroes who wished to find work with the
railroads therefore concentrated in Montreal."[13] In addition to the American Blacks there also were immigrants from the West Indies who arrived during World
War I and whose numbers greatly increased after the
mid-1960s. Between 1960 and 1980 immigration to
Canada from the West Indies averaged 10,000 per
year, and these immigrants must be among the 6,000
English mother tongue Blacks listed in the 1981 census
as hailing from various parts of North and South
America. In addition, the 1981 census listed 3,000
English speakers of African origin living in Quebec.[14]

Less numerous, but more easily counted thanks to
the questions asked in the census, are the English
speakers of Chinese origin who have further added to
the racial diversity of English-speaking Quebec. Under
the pressure of restrictive immigration legislation, by
1951 the Chinese population of Quebec had not even
doubled its 1901 figure of roughly 1,000. Rules that
discouraged the immigration of Chinese families resulted in the presence of a population that was largely
made up of men. These rules began to change in the
late 1940s, so that the Chinese population of Montreal
increased from less than 2,000 in 1951 to nearly 5,000
in 1961, and to nearly 20,000 in 1981. Most of this
population still had a mother tongue from its country

---

13. Robin Winks, *The Blacks in Canada: A History* (New Haven, 1971),
    p. 332.
14. James Walker. *A History of Blacks in Canada: A Study Guide for Teachers
    and Students* (Ottawa, 1980).

of origin, but there were 3,500 English speakers to add a further element of diversity to the English-speaking population.[15]

The final non-British group to be discussed in regard to the changing composition of the English-speaking population did not require passage from another land to Quebec in the post-Confederation era. Between 1931 and 1981 Quebecers of French origin consistently constituted the largest English-speaking group after the British, their numbers growing from 12,000 in 1931 to more than 100,000 fifty years later. Given the manner in which ethnicity has been defined in the census, some of these 100,000 Quebecers were probably the children of families whose paternal line led back to France but which had long functioned in English. There is other information to indicate, however, that the same economic factors that drew post-war immigrants into the English-speaking population also had their effect upon the French origin population. The 1971 census indicated, for instance, that there were 49,000 English mother tongue Quebecers who identified French as the language used most often at home; by contrast there were nearly 75,000 people with French as their mother tongue who gave English as the language used most often at home. In the next generation, these French mother tongue (and most likely French origin) Quebecers were likely to pass English along as the mother tongue of their children. Bill 101 was designed, in part, to block the easy movement of French speakers into the English stream. By the 1970s, with the decline of the birth rate among the French-speaking population and with the willingness of the State to act in such matters, legislation was passed to counter the economic attractions that the English language had presented to non-English-speakers throughout the post-Confederation period.

15. Harry Con et al., *From China to Canada* (Toronto, 1982).

3. Conclusion

If one had encountered ten representative English-speaking Quebecers at the time of Confederation, five would most likely have been Irish, three English and two Scottish. By the time of the 1980 referendum on sovereignty-association, however, the situation would have changed so drastically that only six of the ten would still have been of British origin, and of these six four would have been English. The other four would have derived from a variety of non-British origins. There most likely would have been two French Canadians, a Jew and an Italian. These changes constituted a major transformation in the ethnic composition of English-speaking Quebec and had at their source a variety of economic circumstances. But while there was an economic basis for these changes, there were also important implications for the social and political role of English speakers within Quebec. Without any common ethnic tradition to unite it, the post-Confederation English-speaking population had even less to hold it together than had been the case for those who had lived in Quebec prior to 1867.

SELECT BIBLIOGRAPHY

Caldwell, Gary. *A Demographic Profile of the English-Speaking Population of Quebec, 1921-1971.* Quebec, 1974.

Charbonneau, Hubert et Robert Maheu. *Les aspects démographiques de la question linguistique.* Quebec, 1973.

Lachapelle, Réjean and Jacques Henripin. *The Demolinguistic Situation in Canada.* Montreal, 1982.

Reynolds, Lloyd. *The British Immigrant.* Toronto, 1935.

VII

The Decline
of English-Speaking Quebec
Outside Montreal

Along with the transformation of the ethnic composition of English-speaking Quebec, the other major demographic change that affected this population in the post-Confederation era pertained to its geographical distribution across the province. In 1861 English speakers were already more concentrated in the Montreal area than was the case for Quebecers in general. While 25 % of English speakers resided in the metropolitan area, the figure was only 21 % for all Quebecers. This gap steadily widened in the post-Confederation period until, in 1981, 73 % of all English speakers were living in Montreal as opposed to 44 % for the entire population of the province.[1]

This ever widening gap was caused by two factors. First, the English-speaking population was much more dependent than the French-speaking majority upon the steady arrival of immigrants to contribute to its growth. Since these post-Confederation immigrants tended to settle in Montreal, this led to the greater concentration of English speakers in this one region of the province. This concentration was also caused by

---

1. See Table 1.3.

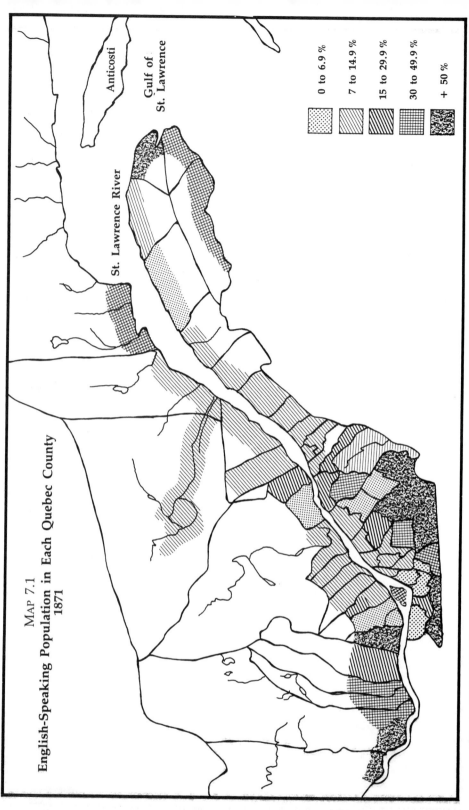

MAP 7.1

English-Speaking Population in Each Quebec County
1871

St. Lawrence River

Anticosti

Gulf of
St. Lawrence

0 to 6.9 %

7 to 14.9 %

15 to 29.9 %

30 to 49.9 %

+ 50 %

Source: Hubert Charbonneau et Robert Maheu, *Les aspects démographiques de la question linguistique* (Québec, 1973).

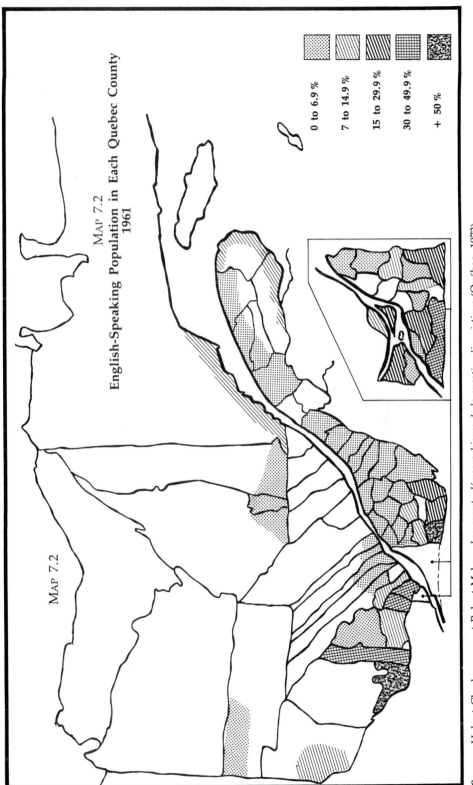

MAP 7.2

English-Speaking Population in Each Quebec County
1961

0 to 6.9 %

7 to 14.9 %

15 to 29.9 %

30 to 49.9 %

+ 50 %

Source: Hubert Charbonneau et Robert Maheu, *Les aspects démographiques de la question linguistique* (Québec, 1973).

the absolute decline of the English-speaking population outside Montreal between 1861 and 1981. During this period the number of Quebecers living outside the city increased by over 300 %, but for English speakers the population outside Montreal actually declined from 198,913 to 191,925. Accordingly, the entire natural increase of this population was lost, most of it through the departure of English speakers for other parts of North America. While most of these English speakers left the province, some settled in Montreal thus further contributing to the concentration of the English-speaking population there.

Of the various regions of the province with significant English-speaking populations only the Ottawa Valley, aside from the Montreal region, registered a significant absolute increase during the post-Confederation period. However, in all of the outlying regions of the province shown in Table 7.1, there was a decline in the percentage of the local population that had English as its mother tongue between 1861 and 1981. This situation resulted in a loss of political power for the English-speaking population in each region, and contributed to the difficulties that had to be faced in maintaining English-language institutions such as schools. This decline is pictorially presented in Maps 7.1 and 7.2 which indicate the virtual disappearance between 1871 and 1961 of Quebec counties with English-speaking majorities. This was a problem that affected all English speakers from the Gaspé to the Ottawa Valley, but, as shall be seen throughout this chapter, the precise causes for the demographic problems faced by English speakers outside Montreal varied considerably from region to region.

TABLE 7.1

Regional Distribution of English-Speaking Quebecers:
Selected Years, 1861-1981

A: English-Speaking Population of Each Region	1861	1871	1901	1931	1971	1981
Montreal	64,531	66,062	126,185	282,456	587,095	514,195
Eastern Townships	89,748	77,789	74,141	57,933	57,830	55,275
Ottawa Valley	34,612	35,669	41,755	35,561	50,525	51,075
Quebec City	30,656	22,730	13,746	12,084	16,005	13,195
Gaspé	11,972	12,252	15,830	18,037	13,880	12,475
B: % of Total English-Speaking Population in Each Region						
Montreal	25	27	44	65	74	73
Eastern Townships	34	32	26	13	7	8
Ottawa Valley	13	15	15	8	6	7
Quebec City	17	9	5	3	2	2
Gaspé	5	5	5	4	2	2
C: English Speakers as % of Regional Population						
Montreal	28	27	27	25	22	18
Eastern Townships	58	46	32	18	11	9
Ottawa Valley	64	53	37	23	18	16
Quebec City	39	29	15	7	4	3
Gaspé	25	21	17	12	6	6

Source: *Census of Canada.*

1. Quebec City

What happened to the English-speaking population of the Quebec City area during the 1860s foreshadowed trends that would occur elsewhere in the province during the post-Confederation period. The region's English-speaking population was reduced by more than one-quarter in the course of a decade, in the process lowering the English-speaking percentage of the local population from 39 % to 29 %. The collapse of the timber trade and the shipbuilding industry in the Quebec City area provoked the departure of these English speakers and contributed to the absolute decline of the province's English-speaking population in the course of the 1860s.

In the absence of any reversal of the economic factors that had started the decline of the English-speaking population, departures continued into the last third of the nineteenth century, resulting in a further 40 % decline in the number of English speakers in the vicinity between 1871 and 1901. As economic activity came to be concentrated in Montreal and points west, Quebec City, like other eastern cities, fell into relative decline, and while some French speakers chose to leave for better job opportunities in New England or Montreal, their numbers did not fall off as did those for English speakers who were willing to resettle anywhere in North America. The continued decline of Quebec City's economic power was evident in the fate of locally based banks which were under the control of English speakers. At the time of Confederation there were two such banks with headquarters in Quebec City, the Quebec Bank and the Union Bank of Lower Canada, both of which moved their head office operations elsewhere early in the 1900s. The Quebec Bank moved the office of its general manager to Montreal in 1912, while the Union Bank shifted its headquarters to Winnipeg in the same year to stay in closer touch with its business which was concentrated in that part of the country. As for a third English-controlled bank in the city, the Stadacona Bank, it lasted only from 1874 to 1876.

By the end of the century, the number of English speakers in the Quebec City area was slightly more than 13,000 and throughout the 1900s this figure changed only marginally. This stabilizing of the population should not be seen, however, in an overly positive light for it meant that the natural increase of the population was lost across the first eight decades of the century. While the population of the region increased dramatically during these years, the English-speaking population remained unchanged, owing both to a continued movement of English speakers from the region and, more significantly, the emergence of a substantial British origin population with French as its mother tongue. In the face of a reduced English-speaking population, those who remained often had difficulty in finding English-speaking partners. Since most of the English speakers of the region were Catholic, the logical alternative was to marry French Catholics, and the children of these marriages were frequently recorded as being of British origin with French as their mother tongue. Indeed, by the time of the 1971 census roughly half of the area's British origin population claimed French as its mother tongue, thus giving support to the assertion of Hubert Charbonneau and Robert Maheu that "les Britanniques de Québec sont en voie d'assimilation rapide; c'est là un phénomène à peu près unique au Québec."[2]

---

2. Hubert Charbonneau et Robert Maheu, *Les aspects démographiques de la question linguistique* (Quebec, 1973), p. 89.

Fishermen in the Gaspé
(Public Archives of Canada, PA-48221)

2. The Gaspé

The economic basis for the Quebec City economy, the timber trade, collapsed in the 1860s and precipitated the rapid decline of the local English-speaking population. In the Gaspé region a similar process took place, but in this case the decline began in the 1930s. Because the traditional fishing economy of the Gaspé remained largely intact, the English-speaking population of the region actually increased by 47 % between 1871 and 1931; only Montreal of the other regions with significant English-speaking populations experienced an absolute increase across those years.

The irony of the persistence of the English-speaking population in the Gaspé was that it was linked to its continued exploitation by the truck system in general and the firm of Charles Robin and Company in particular. As we saw in Chapter III, English-speaking fishermen in outports along the Gaspé coast traditionally committed themselves to selling their catch to the Robin firm in return for the credit the firm provided. This system provided little opportunity for the fishermen to achieve economic independence. Indeed, they frequently had to combine farming and lumbering with fishing to make ends meet. The advantage of the system, however, was that it permitted them to live their lives in a community which was overwhelmingly English. Geographer Roger Clarke was able to find five such towns roughly 90 % of whose total population was English-speaking in 1931.[3] For all communities along the Gulf coast between the towns of Gaspé and Percé 51 % of the population was still English-speaking at the start of the 1930s.

---

3. Roger Clarke, "In Them Days: The Breakdown of a Traditional Fishing Economy in an English Village on the Gaspé Coast", Ph.D. Thesis, McGill University, 1973.

This situation began to change, however, by the 1920s and 1930s as co-operatives emerged to alter the structure of the local economy. These co-operatives, normally operated by French speakers, increasingly controlled the region's fishing activities, centralizing them in a number of centres where French speakers were in the majority. The English-speaking population, if it wished to stay involved in the economy, had to move outside of its small enclaves and work in French. English speakers were faced with a similar challenge with the rise of large-scale mining and lumbering operations where the language of work was frequently French. As one group of historians has written, "La régionalisation des activités économiques entraîne une minorisation du groupe anglophone au sein de l'ensemble francophone très majoritaire qui s'approprie les leviers de décisions régionales." Significantly, while the traditional economy began to deteriorate, one also saw the English-speaking population begin to decline because of "le départ massif des jeunes."[4] Along the Gulf coast only one-third of the population was still English-speaking by 1961. For the region as a whole, a steady decline resulted in the loss of nearly one-third of the 1931 population by 1981.

Between 1931 and 1961 this decline had the same characteristics as the situation in Quebec City in the late nineteenth century; in the face of a changing economic situation many of the more mobile English speakers of the region simply left. Between 1961 and 1981 the decline in the number of English speakers continued, but it was part of a general movement out of the region of all Gaspesians regardless of language. In fact, during the 1960s the population of the region declined by 12 % while the figure for English speakers was only 9 %.

---

4. Bélanger, *Histoire de la Gaspésie*, pp. 562, 665.

English speakers may have joined their French-speaking neighbours in leaving the Gaspé, but for those English speakers that remained there were certain problems not experienced by the linguistic majority. In the Gaspé, as had been the case in the Quebec City area, English speakers faced increased difficulty in finding marriage partners with the same mother tongue once the exodus from the region had begun. Given the fact that Catholics made up roughly half of the English-speaking population, numerous English-French marriages occurred, many of which produced British origin offspring with French as their mother tongue. This process was reflected in the fact that there were over 17,000 British origin residents of the Gaspé in 1971, but fewer than 14,000 with English as their mother tongue. This apparent assimilation provided another element in the decline of the area's English-speaking population after 1931.

3. Ottawa Valley

The four clusters of English speakers outside Montreal under discussion in this chapter could be divided fairly neatly into two groups. On the one hand, there were the Quebec City and Gaspé regions. Both were located in the eastern half of the province with relatively small English-speaking populations at the time of Confederation, which declined when the traditional source of English-speaking employment dried up. Moreover, both were distant from Montreal and the United States and Ontario borders. Once the English-speaking populations of the two regions began to decline, this isolation encouraged continuation of the process of depopulation since English-language services could not easily be received from nearby areas with large agglomerations of English speakers.[5]

---

5. In the Gaspé the one exception to this rule pertains to those areas near the New Brunswick border.

On the other hand, both the Eastern Townships
and the Ottawa Valley could boast English-speaking
populations that made up the majority of the local
population in 1861. In the post-Confederation era there
were periods of significant decline in the number of
English speakers in both areas. Nevertheless, the decline was never so significant as to result in a loss of
the numbers needed to maintain a certain level of local
services in English. Services that could not be provided
locally could be secured from Montreal, Ontario or the
New England States.

Geographic considerations were particularly important to the English-speaking population of the
Ottawa Valley, the only region outside Montreal to
have seen an absolute increase in its English-speaking
population between 1861 and 1981. This growth, however, was entirely a result of events that took place
after the Great Depression. Indeed, in the first three
decades of the twentieth century there was an absolute
decline in the English-speaking population of the
Ottawa Valley of 15 %. The majority of the English
speakers in the region were farmers whose families
had come to the area in the pre-Confederation era.
Some were Americans who came to occupy township
land between 1791 and 1812, while others were immigrants from Britain who had arrived in Quebec following the end of the Napoleonic wars. Regardless of their
origins, many of these English speakers and their
children remained in the region through the first three
decades of Confederation, with the result that the
English-speaking population of the Ottawa Valley actually increased between 1871 and 1901. These gains
were lost, however, in the following three decades as
farmers were lured away by either jobs in the cities or
new lands in the prairies. As French speakers frequently acquired the farms of these English speakers, a
strong French majority emerged by 1931 to replace the

English-speaking majority that had existed at the time of Confederation.[6]

The decline of the English-speaking population of the Ottawa Valley might have continued into the post-1931 period had it not been for the fact that Ontario was only a stone's throw away. In the Quebec City and Gaspé regions, once economic factors had prompted the start of the decline of the English-speaking population, there was nothing to stop it; but such was not the case in the Ottawa Valley. The impact of the proximity to Ontario was evident in the retention of an English-speaking majority in the county of Pontiac. In fact, in the 1981 census Pontiac County held the distinction of being the only one in the province with an English-speaking majority, a situation that was closely linked to the wide array of services that could be secured from the other side of the river. It is little wonder then that some residents of Pontiac County proposed its annexation to Ontario following the election of the Parti québécois in 1976.

In the case of Pontiac County proximity to Ontario resulted in a freeze on rural depopulation, but the Ontario connection functioned in a completely different way to contribute to the growth of the area's English-speaking population by more than 20 % between 1931 and 1981. Following World War II there was a significant expansion of the federal civil service based largely in Ottawa, and as people were drawn to the region seeking employment, some English speakers found themselves settling in newly built suburbs on the Quebec side of the Ottawa River. By 1961 Ottawa suburbs such as Aylmer and Gatineau were home to 11,600 people of British origin, or nearly 30 % of all such people in the area.[7] By 1976 Aylmer and Gatineau had larger English mother tongue popula-

6. Blanchard, *L'Ouest du Canada-français*, II, p. 93.
7. Richard Joy, *Languages in Conflict* (Ottawa, 1967), pp. 100-101.

tions than any other municipalities in the province outside the Montreal area. In contrast with the situation everywhere else in Quebec, these communities drew residents from other parts of Canada instead of losing their numbers to other provinces.[8] In almost every regard the situation in the Ottawa Valley was exceptional. Here, economic prospects generated a growth in the English-speaking population. It is important to note, however, that these improved economic conditions were a product of developments beyond the boundaries of Quebec, and were therefore meaningless to English speakers living outside of the Ottawa Valley.

4.   The Eastern Townships

The most dramatic decline to beset the English-speaking population outside Montreal took place in the Eastern Townships.[9] In 1861 not only did English-speaking Townshippers constitute a majority of the local population, but they also formed the largest regional concentration of English speakers in Quebec. While there were nearly 65,000 English speakers in the Montreal area the figure approached 90,000 in the Eastern Townships. Beginning in the 1860s, however, this situation quickly changed. The region's English-speaking population declined by 13 % during the decade, before stabilizing around the 75,000 figure until the end of the century. Then, between 1901 and 1931, a further 22 % decline took place, following which the population remained steady at roughly 55,000 until 1981. By the start of the 1980s English-speaking Townshippers made up only 9 % of the local population and only 8 % of all English speakers in Quebec.

8. Gary Caldwell, *Le Québec anglophone hors de la région de Montréal dans les années soixante-dix* (Quebec, 1980), pp. 54, 68.

9. As was noted earlier in this study, the Eastern Townships region has been defined to include Huntingdon County, the home of Robert Sellar.

As befits the most significant regional decline of an English-speaking population, the situation that occurred in the Eastern Townships was described in one of the most important books ever written on the history of English-speaking Quebec. In 1907 the first edition of Robert Sellar's *The Tragedy of Quebec* appeared. Sellar was the moving force behind the establishment of the *Huntingdon Gleaner* in the 1860s. As he noted in the preface to his book: "When I came to Huntingdon in 1863 the county was as solidly Protestant as any in Ontario." By 1907, however, Sellar had "witnessed the decline of the Protestant population to the point of being in the minority. The same change, only in a more marked degree, [had] taken place in all the counties east of the Richelieu."[10]

Sellar emphasized the decline of the Protestant population, and not that of those whose mother tongue was English. Indeed, his book was subtitled, "the expulsion of the Protestant farmers", for he was convinced that a conspiracy directed from the Vatican was at the root of the problems in the area. Following the Constitutional Act of 1791 the lands in this area had been divided into townships which were to be free of the burdens of seigneurial tenure. In the seigneurial lands the church had the right to use the force of law to exact tithes from all Catholics. This right had been extended, illegally according to Sellar, to the townships so as to drive the Protestants from the region. Sellar claimed, without a shred of evidence, that the Church financed the purchase of lands from Protestants so that their places might be taken by the tithe-paying Catholics.

Sellar's conviction that dark Papist plots were afoot might seem bizarre to our late twentieth century sensitivities, but, as has already been noted, religion

---

10. Sellar, p. 8.

Robert Sellar
(Robert Sellar, *History of the County of Huntingdon*)

was a major divisive force in the nineteenth century. Moreover, Sellar was in good company in seeing the decline of the English-speaking population in conspiratorial terms. For instance, he was joined in this perception by Richard William Heneker, who in the second half of the nineteenth century was a major business figure in the region. Both Heneker and Sellar believed that the Quebec government was working to further the goals of the Church. Accordingly, the establishment of societies to support French Canadian settlement in the region was frowned upon, particularly when these societies were supported by the provincial government.[11] As Heneker put it: "Every day an aggressive movement is made to swat us all out or to place us in such a position of inferiority that we shall quit in disgust."[12]

This hypersensitivity to the shift in demographic dominance in the region was perhaps to be expected given the power of the English-speaking Townshippers at the middle of the nineteenth century. Prior to the decline of the 1860s these people had established their own university, Bishop's, and their own bank, the Eastern Townships Bank. Now that those glory days were gone Townshippers not only wrote about the problem, as Sellar did, but they also acted to try to halt the flow of events. Some of these actions were simply symbolic ones designed to show the anger of local English speakers.

The most notable of such acts pertained to the difficulties of Donald Morrison, better known as the Megantic outlaw.[13] In 1886 Morrison's father lost his

---

11. Little, "Watching the Frontier Disappear".
12. Public Archives of Canada (PAC), British American Land Company Papers (BAL), Vol. VI, Hencker to J.H. Pope, 18 August 1882.
13. The Morrison case has been treated, for instance, in two fairly recent works. Bernard Epps, *The Outlaw of Megantic* (Toronto, 1973); Clarke Wallace, *Wanted: Donald Morrison* (Toronto, 1977).

farm to a local money lender, who in turn sold it to a French-speaking family. In anger over these events Morrison assaulted the money lender, fired a bullet into the home of the French-speaking family, and killed a deputy who had come to arrest him. From June 1888 to March 1889 Morrison was pursued by the provincial police, but to no avail. During this period he was openly harboured by the predominantly Scottish residents of the Lake Megantic region who considered him a hero. A "Donald Morrison Defense Fund" was established, and at least one militia unit committed itself to his protection.[14] When he was finally brought to trial, Morrison received an 18 year sentence for manslaughter for killing the deputy.

Morrison may have lost his case, but for English-speaking residents of the region he provided a cause around which a former majority might rally. Townshippers were prepared to ignore the fact that the French-speaking family which had legally acquired the Morrison farm had been assaulted and its barn mysteriously burned down. During his ten months as a fugitive, Morrison gave these people the opportunity to thumb their noses at the government of Honoré Mercier by harbouring a man that the premier badly wanted captured. This act of defiance was particularly significant since Mercier was perceived as a staunch supporter of French settlement in the region.

When not engaged in symbolic acts such as the defense of Donald Morrison, English-speaking Townshippers tried to seek more practical means of regaining their lost majority. In particular, efforts were made to recruit immigrants from Britain to settle in the area. However, attempts such as the establishment in the 1880s of the Eastern Townships Colonization Society ultimately came to naught. The lands that were still

---

14. Archives nationales du Québec, Ministère de la Justice, Vol. XCII, f. 4313, M.W. McMinn to Attorney General, 18 November 1889; Vol. LXXXVI, f. 1107, Attorney General to A.P. Caron, 10 August 1888.

available in the region were not of sufficiently high
quality to draw immigrants to the region. In fact, the
superior quality of western lands, and not any papist
conspiracy, stood at the heart of the decline of the
region's English-speaking population between 1861
and 1931.

The relative economic decline of the Eastern
Townships was visible, however, not only in the preference of its English-speaking farmers for western
lands; it was also evident in the loss of economic
power by the region's most powerful English-speaking
businessmen. This loss of power was particularly evident in the career of Richard William Heneker. Heneker came to the region from Britain in 1855 to succeed
Alexander Galt as the commissioner of the British
American Land Company, the proprietor of much of
the land in the Eastern Townships. To this position of
power Heneker had, by the 1870s, added the presiden-
cies of the Eastern Townships Bank and the Paton
Manufacturing Company whose woollen mill at Sherbrooke was the city's largest employer. Before his
retirement to Britain in 1902, Heneker also served as
mayor of Sherbrooke, chancellor of Bishop's University, and founder and first president of the Sherbrooke
Protestant Hospital. Heneker was involved with nearly
every activity of interest to the region's English-
speaking population. Nevertheless, he departed in
1902 a disillusioned man.

In part, Heneker's displeasure was a product of
the fifty years of demographic change though which
he had lived. He suffered, for instance, through the
growing power of French speakers within the Sherbrooke municipal government. He was particularly
displeased by the ascendancy of a French speaker to
the mayor's chair for the first time in the 1880s, even
though a French-speaking majority had existed in
Sherbrooke since the early 1870s. This delay was in no

small part Heneker's doing. He saw to it that the city council retained the right to choose the mayor until 1898 and that the English-speaking sections of the city were over-represented in the council until 1889. Heneker strongly resented complaints from French-speaking leaders during the 1870s that such a system was unjust. He not very diplomatically reminded them "that if they [had] a majority of Sherbrooke's population it [was] because those who differ[ed] from them in origin [had] invested capital and energy in the development of the resources of the town, thus furnishing homes and work to those who would otherwise [have been] expatriated."[15]

Heneker's power was not only circumscribed by the emergence of a French majority in the region, even though he frequently spoke as if that were his only problem. He also was the victim of the concentration of power within the Canadian economy in the hands of fewer and fewer men whose operations were normally based in either Montreal or Toronto. As his woollen mill required more capital, it came under the control of Montreal businessmen; and the railway in which he held an interest was taken over by the Montreal based CPR.[16] But the clearest sign of the decline in the fortunes of businessmen from the Townships came with the demise of the Eastern Townships Bank. By the time of Heneker's retirement the bank had already begun to stray from its original vocation as an institution designed to serve the interests of the region. In its first decades of operation most of the bank's investments were in the region, frequently to assist English-speaking farmers and businessmen. As this market shrank because of the exodus of English-speakers to the west, the bank moved to establish

15. Ronald Rudin. "The Transformation of the Eastern Townships of Richard William Heneker", *Journal of Canadian Studies*, XIX (1984).
16. *Ibid.*

offices outside the region, occasionally opening branches in the prairies to serve ex-Townshippers. This expansion put the bank into direct competition with much larger institutions and weakened its financial position. When the Canadian Bank of Commerce made an offer for the acquisition of the Eastern Townships Bank it was accepted, and in 1912 the Sherbrooke-based bank passed from the scene. [17]

The decline of the bank had the practical effect of moving economic decisionmaking from Sherbrooke to Toronto and potentially threatened the loss of financing for the affairs of English speakers in the region, providing them with a further incentive to leave. The concentration of economic power in Canada's two major cities also encouraged the departure from Sherbrooke of its most energetic businessmen who, quite naturally, wanted to be nearer the centre of action. It is interesting to note that Heneker's son, Richard Tuson Heneker, went off to Montreal to practice law in the service of such firms as the CPR.

Economic factors such as the attractiveness of western lands and the decline of Sherbrooke as a business centre of importance were at the root of the absolute decline of the English-speaking population of the Eastern Townships by 35 % between 1861 and 1931. Such factors were beyond the comprehension of people like Robert Sellar. Nevertheless, Sellar did appreciate that once the decline began it would be perpetuated by the weakening of local institutions. As Sellar observed, "The situation of the few families who cling to a decaying township settlement is painful... It is with difficulty [that] services in the church are maintained... A day comes when there are too few

---

17. Ronald Rudin, "Naissance et déclin d'une élite locale: La Banque des Cantons de l'Est, 1859-1912," *Revue d'histoire de l'Amérique française,* XXXVIII (1984), pp. 165-179.

families to maintain the school."[18] This weakening of local institutions also played a key role in the decline of the English-speaking population in the Eastern Townships county of Compton. Historian Marcel Bellavance found that by 1900 "the increasingly frequent departures of the members of [the] community had jeopardized the existence of institutions; in turn the weakness of the institutions hastened the departure of those who had remained."[19]

In spite of the problems experienced by English-speaking residents of the Eastern Townships between 1861 and 1931 and in spite of the anguish displayed by some Townshippers, the absolute decline of the population did not continue beyond 1931. Between 1931 and 1981 the number of English speakers in the region remained essentially unchanged, which is to say that the natural increase of the population was lost. Nevertheless, there were aspects of the situation in the Eastern Townships which compared favourably with those in the Gaspé and Quebec City regions during the same period. In the latter two areas the initial decline in the English-speaking population left relatively small populations which were isolated from major concentrations of English settlement. By contrast, with 50,000 residents the English speakers of the Townships could avail themselves of an English-language university, CEGEP, hospital, and daily newspaper. All of these were located in the Sherbrooke-Lennoxville area, and indeed since 1931 there has been a greater concentration of the area's English speakers in the vicinity of Sherbrooke because of both the services and employment available there.[20]

---

18. Sellar, pp. 218-219.
19. Marcel Bellavance, *A Village in Transition: Compton, Quebec, 1880-1920* (Ottawa, 1982), p. 27.
20. W.G. Ross, *Three Eastern Townships Mining Villages Since 1863* (Lennoxville, 1975).

The presence of 50,000 English speakers largely concentrated within a relatively small area of the Townships also played a role in the marriage patterns of this population. In the Quebec City and Gaspé regions marriages between English and French speakers influenced the decline of the local English-speaking populations. However, the conditions that existed in these two regions were not present in the Eastern Townships where English speakers had a greater choice of partners with the same mother tongue. Moreover, the English-speaking population of the Eastern Townships was predominantly Protestant, thus further working against English-French marriages. Accordingly, there was no evidence of the assimilation of the British origin population into the French stream in the 1971 census. In both the Quebec City and Gaspé regions the number of people of British origin exceeded the number with English as their mother tongue. By contrast, in 1971 there were 55,530 Townshippers of British origin and 57,830 with English as their mother tongue. Evidently, the region was even home to a number of people whose mother tongue was English but who were not of British origin, and this was an indication of the relative strength of the English language in the area.

In the absence of a profound economic change such as that experienced in the Ottawa Valley following the expansion of the federal government, the English-speaking population of the Eastern Townships is unlikely to grow. Nevertheless, with 50,000 members, sound community institutions, and relatively easy access to Montreal, the English-speaking population in the Townships appeared at the start of the 1980s more likely to hold its own than the English-speaking enclaves in the eastern half of the province.

5. Conclusion

Just as economic factors played a central role in the population movements described in the previous chapter, so too did such concerns influence the fortunes of the English-speaking populations in the various regions of the province outside Montreal. All four regions discussed here experienced declines in their English-speaking populations at one time or another during the post-Confederation era. The precise timing of these losses varied, however, depending upon economic circumstances. In Quebec City and in the Eastern Townships the process began in the 1860s; in the Ottawa Valley it was in the first years of the 1900s, while in the Gaspé the decline began in the 1930s. In only one of the regions was there a significant increase in the English-speaking population during the post-Confederation period. This occurred in the Ottawa Valley, and was once again linked to economic circumstances.

A variety of non-economic factors, such as the strength of English-language institutions or the religious makeup of the local English-speaking population, were capable of either slowing down or accelerating the decline in the number of English speakers within any given region once the exodus had begun. However, the decline of English-speaking Quebec outside Montreal was basically caused by economic conditions. Given the ease with which they could go to other parts of North America, English speakers made a habit of moving on when better economic prospects existed elsewhere. As shall be shown in the next chapter, the absolute decline of the English-speaking population finally reached Montreal by the 1970s. This decline, like the others that had preceded it, was strongly influenced by economic factors.

SELECT BIBLIOGRAPHY

Bélanger, Jules, et al. *Histoire de la Gaspésie.* Montreal, 1981.

Caldwell, Gary. *Le Québec anglophone hors de la région de Montréal dans les années soixante-dix.* Quebec, 1980.

Joy, Richard. *Languages in Conflict.* Ottawa, 1967.

Little, J.I. "Watching the Frontier Disappear: English-Speaking Reaction to French Canadian Colonization in the Eastern Townships, 1844-1890.", *Journal of Canadian Studies,* XV (1980-1), 93-111.

Rudin, Ronald. "The Transformation of the Eastern Townships of Richard William Heneker, 1855-1902", *Journal of Canadian Studies,* XIX (1984), 32-49.

Sellar, Robert. *The Tragedy of Quebec.* Toronto, 1974.

VIII

English-Speaking Quebec and The Montreal Economy

The century following Confederation saw the steady growth of the English-speaking population residing in the Montreal area. Between 1871 and 1971 the number of English speakers in the area grew from 66,000 to nearly 600,000 as a result of the steady influx of both immigrants from abroad and English speakers from the outlying regions of the province. Both groups came to the city to avail themselves of certain economic opportunities. Even if the immigrants did not always come to the city with English as their mother tongue, economic circumstances frequently pushed them to learn English and then pass it on to their children. There was a general recognition that economic success could only be achieved in Montreal through the use of English, and as long as the Montreal economy was strong it seemed likely to attract an ever-growing number of English speakers to the city.

During the decade of the 1970s, however, the century of steady growth for the English-speaking population of Montreal came to an end, for there was an absolute decline in the number of English speakers of 12 %. There were nearly 75,000 fewer English speakers in the Montreal region in 1981 than there had been ten years earlier. This decline was closely related to economic changes whose roots stretched back several decades. Just as the earlier expansion of the English-speaking population had been tied to the health of the Montreal economy and the strength of the English language within that economy, now the decline reflected a reversal of those characteristics. As employment prospects for English speakers dried up, leaving the province became an increasingly attractive option, just as it had been to English speakers in other parts of the province. The net loss of English-speaking Montrealers to other provinces was already substantial by the mid-1960s, but this loss was counterbalanced by the natural growth of the population and the linguistic decisions of Quebecers whose mother tongue was not English to pass English on to their children. By the 1970s, however, the scale of the exodus was so great that nothing could prevent an absolute decline in the English-speaking population of the city.

The rise and fall of the English-speaking population of Montreal was closely related to the evolution of the local economy. During the first half century after Confederation the English-speaking business leaders of Montreal expanded their control over the Canadian economy. In the process they reinforced an economic structure that reserved its best paying positions for English speakers. Although there were numerous English-speaking Montrealers who worked for wages that were insufficient to support a family, the disproportionate representation of English speakers in well-paying jobs led to the situation in 1961 in which an English speaker earned 50 % more than the average French-speaking Montrealer. Between 1960 and 1980, however, this situation changed considerably so that English speakers earned only 14 % more than French speakers in 1981. This change coincided with the decline in the power of the English-speaking elite, a process that had begun in the 1920s. Well paying jobs were increasingly distributed in a different fashion, encouraging both the upward mobility of a number of French speakers and the departure of English-speaking Montrealers. Those who departed tended to be relatively well paid and well educated; those left behind occupied lower paying positions, which depressed the average earnings of English speakers.

The fortunes of the English-speaking population of Montreal were inextricably linked to changes in the structure of the local economy. The sections that follow will therefore emphasize the changing role of English speakers within the Montreal economy in the post-Confederation era.

1.   The Heyday of the Golden Square Mile, 1867-1914

Confederation was, in certain respects, designed by and for the English-speaking business leaders of Montreal. After 1867 all major economic concerns were to be handled by the federal government, and given the power of the Montreal business elite their lobbying in Ottawa was highly successful during the first half century of the new political regime. For instance, the Montreal business leaders had argued strongly for Confederation as a means of facilitating the construction of a trans-continental railway. It is not surprising, therefore, that in the late 1870s a Montreal-based syndicate won the contract to build the CPR with support from the federal government in the form of $25 million and 25 million acres of land. Similarly, the Bank of Montreal, one of the most important English-run institutions in the city, entered the post-Confederation era in a position of influence as the federal government's banker. From this vantage point it successfully lobbied against proposals that might have increased competition within the banking industry. In addition to their ties with the federal government, English-speaking

business leaders also profited from other circumstances in the pre-World War I period, some of which
would no longer exist in the post-war era. They benefited, for instance, from close ties with investors in
Britain. The British connection had been crucial to the
English-speaking business elite ever since the Conquest, and this continued to be the case after 1867 as
Britain remained the major source of foreign investment in Canada. Both the CPR and the Bank of
Montreal profited from British investment, as did industries such as the Vickers shipyards.

During the pre-World War I era the Montreal
business elite was also aided by the city's geographical
location. Montreal's site had originally been chosen in
the seventeenth century because it was the farthest
point inland before the first major rapids in the St.
Lawrence River were encountered. Following the
deepening of the ship channel between Montreal and
Quebec City in the 1840s and 1850s and the building of
the CPR in the 1880s, Montreal was able to take full
advantage of its location. The grain produced by
prairie farmers was sent east by rail and then from
Montreal to Liverpool by ship; imported goods, many
of which were destined for the households of the same
prairie farmers, came to Montreal by ship before being
loaded on the CPR. Accordingly, Montreal served as
the hub of two different forms of transportation.

These various advantages were put to good use by
the English-speaking elite of Montreal to extend its
control over the Canadian economy in the years immediately preceding World War I. These years saw the
concentration of control over the economy in fewer
and fewer hands, and as the leading business figures
in the country the Montrealers were active participants
in the merger movement. The CPR took over many
smaller lines, while the Bank of Montreal and the
Royal Bank played active roles in reducing competition

within the banking industry. New firms were also created during this period under the influence of Montreal financiers such as Herbert Holt and Max Aitken (later Lord Beaverbrook), who combined existing companies to create new ones. Holt provided himself with a monopoly over the provision of gas and electricity in Montreal through the formation of Montreal Light, Heat and Power in 1901, while Aitken came to dominate the Canadian cement industry with the founding of Canada Cement in 1909.

So great was the power of this small cluster of English-speaking Montrealers that it was described by Stephen Leacock as having "enjoyed a prestige in that era that not even the rich deserved."[1] The mansions of the English elite were concentrated within an area referred to as the Golden Square Mile, whose residents were estimated to have controlled 70 % of all Canadian wealth at the turn of the century. One of those mansions, the home of the CPR'S William Cornelius Van Horne, was supposed to have had an art collection that would have been "the envy of museums around the world."[2]

The residents of the Golden Square Mile constituted only a small percentage of the more than 150,000 English speakers who lived in Montreal at the beginning of World War I, but the impact of the elite was strongly felt by those who made up the majority of the English speakers. For instance, there were the skilled labourers who were frequently recruited from Britain by members of the elite to work in the city's industries. These men were reasonably well paid, but the same could not be said of those English speakers who worked for the city's elite as unskilled labour in the factories of Montreal.

1. Stephen Leacock, *Leacock's Montreal* (Toronto, 1963), pp. 233-235.
2. Jean-Claude Marsan, *Montreal in Evolution* (Montreal, 1981), p. 258.

St. James Street, Montreal, 1920
(Public Archives of Canada, PA-123784)

Ravenscrag, the Montreal residence of Sir Hugh Allan
(Public Archives of Canada, PA-45895)

The plight of such English speakers was described in Herbert Ames' 1897 book *The City Below The Hill.* Ames concentrated upon an area to the southwest of Old Montreal which was inhabited by 38,000 people. Most of the families there were united by a dependence upon wage-labour even though they came from various ethnic backgrounds. Ames chose to examine this part of town so as "to study a class rather than a race."[3] The working-class families of this area were rarely able to afford more than the poorest of housing for themselves. As historians Bettina Bradbury and Terry Copp have shown, between 1860 and the onset of the Great Depression, the English-speaking families of this region of the city were rarely able to survive on a single wage.[4] Wives and children were sent into the labour force to supplement the wage of the husband, but this only served to depress the already low wages being paid.

The personal reactions of these English speakers to their lot were made public in testimony during the 1880s before a federal royal commission looking into the relations between capital and labour. One witness before the commission was Eli Massy, an English-speaking cigar maker who worked as an unskilled labourer. Massy earned $7.00 per week, out of which $1.50 was set aside for rent, $.80 for fuel, and $4.00 for food He admitted that with his two children he really needed at least $5.00 for food. Asked directly whether his family could live on $7.00 per week, he emphatically responded, "No sir."[5] Families such as the Massys consequently resorted to a wide variety of strategies to survive. While Mrs. Van Horne was tending her art collection, Mrs. Massy was probably tending the pigs,

3. Copp, p. 15.
4. Bradbury, "The Family Economy"; Copp, *Anatomy of Poverty.*
5. Greg Kealey, ed., *Canada Investigates Industrialism* (Toronto, 1973), p. 213.

taking in boarders, or leaving children who could not be fed in orphanages.[6]

While life was difficult for wage earning English speakers, it is important, nevertheless, to realize that these people did have some advantages that were not available to their French-speaking counterparts. There were, for instance, a variety of institutions which were supported by the wealth of the business elite, which operated in English, and which were as a result more accessible to the English-speaking working class. A case in point was the Royal Edward Chest Hospital, established in 1909 by one of the city's wealthier English-speaking families. Since the hospital operated in English, it no doubt contributed to the generally lower level of tuberculosis among English-speaking Montrealers than was found among French speakers.[7] In addition, there were employment prospects for members of English-speaking working class families that did not exist for French speakers. As described in Chapter III, daughters of English-speaking families could more readily secure employment as maids in the mansions of the Golden Square Mile, thus easing the burdens at home. In the post-World War I era there was even some evidence of upward mobility for English-speaking workers that did not exist among Montreal's French-speaking population.

---

6. Bettina Bradbury, "The Fragmented Family: Family Strategies in the Face of Death, Illness and Poverty", in Joy Parr, ed., *Childhood and Family in Canadian History* (Toronto, 1982), pp. 109-128.

7. Robert Sweeney, "A Brief Sketch of the Economic History of English-Speaking Quebec", in Caldwell and Waddell, eds, *The English of Quebec*, p. 90.

TABLE 8.1

Clerical, Professional and Managerial Employment:
British and French Male Quebecers,
1931-1981

ETHNIC ORIGIN	% NON-AGRICULTURAL WORKERS IN CLERICAL, PROFESSIONAL OR MANAGERIAL JOBS				
	1931	1941	1961	1971	1981
British	30 %	42	46	39	40
French	12 %	22	22	25	29
British-French	+18	+20	+24	+16	+11

Source: *Census of Canada.*

2. The Beginning of Change, 1914-1960

The period from the start of the first World War to
the beginning of the Quiet Revolution was one of
change for both wage-earning English speakers and
their wealthier co-linguists who lived on the flanks of
Mt. Royal. For the first group there was considerable
evidence of improvement in economic status. This
period saw the creation of numerous clerical, professional and managerial positions in the Quebec economy which were particularly concentrated in Montreal.
Many of these jobs were in firms which were under
the control of the English-speaking business elite
which catered to a market that spanned all of Canada.
These new posts tended to be reserved for people who
could function in English, giving considerable advantages to English speakers. As Table 8.1 indicates, both
the British and French origin populations of the province saw an increasingly large percentage of their
workforce employed in such occupations between 1931
and 1961. However, the gap between the two groups,

which was already considerable in 1931, grew even larger during the three following decades.[8]

Given the fact that immigration from Britain was relatively insignificant during the three decades from 1931 to 1961, the increase in the number of men of British origin in these jobs from 37,000 to 66,000 had to be, in large part, the result of the upward mobility of English speakers whose families were already settled in Quebec. In his 1935 study of the British element in Montreal, Lloyd Reynolds found numerous examples of children of British labourers who had moved into various white collar occupations.[9] Similarly, the extent of this inter-generational mobility was made clear by sociologists Yves de Jocas and Guy Rocher in an important 1957 study. The authors used a sample taken from Quebec marriage records of men who married in 1954. These records provided the occupation of the man at the time of his marriage as well as the occupation of his father at the time of the son's birth. By comparing these occupations it was possible to gauge the inter-generational mobility that might have taken place. Jocas and Rocher concluded that "English-speaking sons tended to shift from manual to non-manual occupations to a larger extent and more rapidly than the French.... The sons of the English-speaking unskilled workers will generally enter the public services or the clerical and sales group, while the French in the same situation will generally [only advance to] become skilled workers.... The son of a French skilled worker will enter the clerical group

---

8. Tracing the occupational structure within English-speaking Quebec is no easy matter. The definition of occupations as presented in the census changed considerably over time thus making comparisons difficult. The effort has been made, however, to reduce these inconsistencies as much as possible. Moreover, information regarding the occupations of English mother tongue Quebecers only first became available with the 1981 census. As a result, Table 8.1 presents comparisons between British and French origin Quebecers.

9. Reynolds, *The British Immigrant*, p. 129.

[while] the son of an English-speaking skilled worker will rather enter the top two occupational levels. [i.e. professional and managerial positions]."[10]

While Jocas and Rocher claimed to be addressing themselves to differences between English and French speakers, in fact they defined their terms so as to compare British and French origin Quebecers. As was shown in Chapter VI, by the 1940s and 1950s people of British origin were constituting an ever-diminishing percentage of the English-speaking population, Accordingly, the upward mobility that they found might not have extended to the entire English-speaking population. It would appear, however, from an analysis of the Jewish population that this mobility was experienced by many of the groups that formed part of the English-speaking population of Montreal. In 1931 Quebec's Jews were heavily concentrated in various manufacturing occupations such as the production of clothing. As a result, 32 % of all Jewish males were engaged in manufacturing, while only 10 % were employed in either clerical or professional positions. By 1961 the situation had greatly changed; 20 % of Jewish men were in clerical or professional posts and only 17 % were still in manufacturing.

The upward mobility of English speakers in the post World War II period undoubtedly played a major role in the considerable gap that existed between the wages of English and French-speaking Montrealers when such information was first presented in the 1961 census. Whether this gap was larger or smaller in earlier years can never be known for sure, in the absence of comparable data. However, given information available from studies such as that prepared by Jocas and Rocher, it seems reasonable to conclude that

10. Yves de Jocas and Guy Rocher, "Inter-Generational Mobility in the Province of Quebec", *Canadian Journal of Economics and Political Science*, XXIII (1957), p. 66.

the wage gap between English and French-speaking
Montrealers grew in the decades preceding the Quiet
Revolution.

TABLE 8.2

Average Earnings
of English and French-Speaking Montrealers,
1961-1980

	AVERAGE MALE EARNINGS			
	1961	1970	1977	1980
A: English Speakers	$ 5829	8736	17065	19892
B: French Speakers	3873	6625	14880	17474
B as a % of A	66 %	76 %	87 %	88 %

Source: Jac-André Boulet, *Language and Earnings in Montreal* (Ottawa,
1980); Jac-André Boulet et al, *L'évolution des disparités linguistiques de revenus de travail au Canada de 1970 à 1980* (Ottawa, 1983).

The superior position of English speakers in 1961
did not mean that all English speakers earned more
than their French-speaking counterparts; nor did all
English speakers achieve upward mobility in the decades before 1961. Among the 70 % of male Montreal
workers who earned less than $5,000 in 1961, there
was no difference in the wages earned by English and
French speakers. Rather, the entire gap was the product of the concentration of English speakers in the
city's best jobs, and many of the occupants of these
positions were the upwardly mobile English speakers
of the post-World War II era.[11] In the years after 1961
the disparities between English and French speakers
narrowed as Table 8.2 indicates, and when this occurred it stemmed from changes in the linguistic composition of Montrealers with the best paying jobs. The
basis for this change was already being laid, however,
in the years prior to 1961.

11. Boulet, *Language and Earnings*, p. 26.

Although the period between 1914 and 1961 saw the expansion of firms controlled by Montreal's English-speaking elite, it also saw the relative decline of the power of this elite within the Canadian economy. In the post-World War I era British investment, long an important element in Montreal's powerful position within the economy, declined in importance with its place being taken by investment from the United States. As this latter form of investment tended to be channeled through Toronto, it gave that city a clear advantage over Montreal in the race for primacy in the Canadian economy. Montreal's position was further compromised by the building of the St. Lawrence Seaway which permitted ocean-going ships to pass by its port. As the centre of the Canadian economy shifted to the west, Montreal came to occupy a position similar to that in which Quebec City found itself in the mid-1800s.

There is considerable evidence of Montreal's relative loss of economic power in the post-1914 period. In 1915, for instance, Toronto interests secured for their city a direct link with a transcontinental railway with the completion of the Canadian Northern. It had earlier been an indication of the strength of the Montreal business elite that the CPR main line went nowhere near Toronto. The growing importance of Toronto interests was similarly reflected in the fact that by the 1920s the number of manufacturing employees in that city exceeded the number in Montreal. By the 1930s the value of shares traded on the Toronto Stock Exchange exceeded the value of shares traded on the two Montreal exchanges, and by the start of the 1960s there were more major firms with head offices in Toronto than there were in Montreal. [12]

In the period betwen 1914 and 1960 these changes were merely indicators of a relative decline in the

---

12. Nader, Cities of Canada, I, pp. 213-214.

power held by Montreal's predominantly English-speaking business elite. However, its institutions, such as the Bank of Montreal, continued to expand, in the process giving additional opportunity for employment to English-speaking Montrealers. Nevertheless, at the same time that these institutions were expanding, economic power was steadily shifting to Bay Street from St. James Street. In the post-1960 era political factors combined with the continued erosion of the power of the Montreal elite to trigger a massive exodus of English speakers from the city.

3. Economic Factors and the Exodus of English-Speaking Montrealers, 1960-80

By the early 1960s the impact of the relative decline of the Montreal economy upon the city's English-speaking workforce was already evident. In an article published in 1969, Jacques Dofny and Muriel Garon-Audy replicated the occupational mobility study of Jocas and Rocher that was noted earlier.[13] The first study had compared the occupations of Quebec men married in 1954 with those of their fathers at the time of their sons' births. Dofny and Garon-Audy made the same comparisons, but they selected a sample of men married in 1964. They found that the 1954 situation in which rapid upward mobility was virtually the preserve of English speakers had been completely transformed by the 1960s. Now the French speakers were more likely to move two rungs up the occupational ladder, in stark contrast with the superiority enjoyed by English speakers ten years earlier. A third study pertaining to men married in 1974 only served to indicate the continuation of the trends evident in the 1960s.[14]

13. Jacques Dofny et Muriel Garon-Audy, "Mobilités professionnelles au Québec", *Sociologie et sociétés*, I (1969), pp. 277-301.

14. Muriel Garon-Audy, *Mobilités professionnelles et géographiques au Québec, 1954-64-74* (Montreal, 1982).

Dofny and Garon-Audy attributed the changes they observed to the structural transformations that the Quebec economy was undergoing. On the one hand, there were fewer and fewer managerial, clerical and professional positions for English speakers, given the growing concentration of such employment in Toronto. It was not that new jobs in Montreal's head offices were unavailable for English speakers, but rather that they were no longer being created as rapidly as had earlier been the case, thus limiting the upward mobility of English speakers. On the other hand, the 1960s saw the rapid expansion of white-collar employment in positions funded by the provincial government. These jobs provided the means whereby French speakers could achieve upward mobility more readily than had been the case in the 1950s.

The problems for English speakers who were seeking well-paying jobs within the Montreal economy only grew worse throughout the 1960s and 1970s. English speakers had always benefited from employment prospects in firms that were oriented towards a market that transcended the boundaries of Quebec and in which English was the primary language of business. These were firms that had been controlled by the English-speaking elite but which were offering little in the way of employment possibilities in the post-1960 era. Robert Lacroix and François Vaillancourt found that by 1978 English speakers had an advantage over French speakers only in firms "tournés vers l'extérieur."[15] As a proportion of all employment in the province, however, jobs in the "external" sector declined from 52 % in 1961 to 42 % in 1978. Lacroix and Vaillancourt noted that there were 1.2 workers in the head offices of Montreal-based financial institutions in 1951 for every one worker in Toronto, but by 1972

---

15. Robert Lacroix et François Vaillancourt, *Les revenus et la langue au Québec* (Quebec, 1981), p. 55.

Sun Life Building, Montreal (Archives de la Ville de Montréal)

there were only half as many workers in that sector in Montreal as there were in Toronto. Some firms, such as the Bank of Montreal, transferred a portion of their head office operations to be closer to the centre of decisionmaking in Toronto, while other firms, such as Sun Life, moved all head office jobs there. The result was that between 1967 and 1978 head office employment in Quebec increased by only 8 % while that in regional offices increased by 34 %. This situation evidently aided the upward mobility of French speakers and limited the prospects of English speakers.

The role of political factors cannot be completely excluded from an understanding of the acceleration of Montreal's decline as a centre of head office employment. Clearly, the departure of Sun Life in 1978 was timed to cause embarrassment for the newly elected Parti québécois government. It seems unlikely, however, that Sun Life would have left had Montreal still occupied its earlier powerful role within the Canadian economy. Similarly, many of the English-speaking Montrealers who departed between 1960 and 1980 may have left in part because of the political events of that period. Nevertheless, one has to wonder if they would have left in such numbers had their own prospects for upward mobility not been compromised by the ascendancy of Toronto. It is significant that among those English speakers who left Montreal during the 1970s an important proportion were "primarily unilingual and highly paid."[16] This characteristic is confirmed by the fact that 57 % of all English mother tongue Quebecers who departed between 1976 and 1981 had at least begun university. Among French speakers, only 4 % of those who moved on to other provinces had begun university.[17]

---

16. Boulet, p. 43.
17. Alliance Quebec, *Brief on Demographic Tendencies* (Montreal, 1984), p. 41.

With the loss of upward mobility for English speakers and a greater opportunity for such mobilty among French speakers, the disparities between the incomes of the two groups of Montrealers narrowed considerably between 1960 and 1980. While the average French speaker earned 66 % of what an English speaker earned in 1960, this figure had increased to 88 % by 1980. As Table 8.3 indicates, the disparities between unilingual English speakers and bilingual French speakers were eliminated during this period, reflecting changes within the better paying positions in the economy. Table 8.1 showed the closing of the occupational gap between English and French speakers in white-collar positions, and the figures below corroborate that finding. With the strengthening of the position of French speakers in the best paying jobs in the Montreal economy, the overall disparity between English and French earnings melted away. As we saw earlier, the superior earnings of English speakers among the top 15 % of all male wage earners in Montreal was at the root of the disparity in 1960. Jac-André Boulet has noted that by 1977 "the linguistic earnings disparities [had] almost disappeared at this earnings level."[18]

At the start of the 1960s there was scarcely any difference between English and French-speaking Montrealers occupying the lower paying jobs in the economy. Then, following the 1960s and 1970s there was scarcely any gap among those in better paying positions. This closing of income disparities should not be confused, however, with an equalization of the economic power wielded by the two linguistic groupings. While the power of the Montreal English-speaking business elite declined relative to that of Toronto, within the Quebec economy these English speakers

---

18. Boulet, p. 29.

TABLE 8.3

Male Earnings and Bilingualism:
Montreal, 1961-1980

	1961	1970	1980
English Mother Tongue			
Bilingual	5,931	8,851	19,920
Unilingual	5,749	8,631	19,840
French Mother Tongue			
Bilingual	4,201	7,355	19,411
Unilingual	2,975	5,422	14,351

Source: Jac-André Boulet, *Language and Earnings in Montreal*, (Ottawa, 1980); Jac-André Boulet et al, *L'évolution des disparités linguistiques de revenus de travail au Canada de 1970 à 1980*, (Ottawa, 1983).

still controlled more of the province's productive capacity than their numbers warranted. André Raynauld found that in the 1960s French speakers controlled, for instance, manufacturing firms which employed only 22 % of all workers in that sector in Quebec. According to François Vaillancourt, the Raynauld study was still relevant at the end of the 1970s.[19] With the growth of the provincial bureaucracy, the introduction of language legislation, and the loss of head office employment, an ability to function in French became essential in securing a good paying job within the Montreal economy. This was a major change from the situation that had existed as late as the 1950s. Nevertheless, the changes of the 1960s and 1970s could not liquidate the control over the Quebec economy that Montreal's business elite had exercised since the Conquest.

19. François Vaillancourt, "La Charte de la langue française du Québec: Un essai d'analyse", *Canadian Public Policy*, IV (1978), p. 292.

4. Conclusion

Just as economic concerns influenced the physical mobility of English speakers elsewhere in Quebec, so too did such factors play a central role in the post-Confederation history of English-speaking Montreal. Given their ability to move with relative ease to other parts of North America, English-speaking Montrealers did what their counterparts in the Eastern Townships, the Gaspé and the Quebec City regions had done before them. When economic circumstances took a turn for the worse, they moved on to what they saw as greener pastures. During the 1970s many English-speaking Montrealers saw political factors such as the rise of the Parti québécois and the introduction of language legislation as the key to the exodus that took place. It would be foolish to deny the effects of political insecurity upon people's behaviour. Nevertheless, that insecurity was able to have an impact only because of the changes in the Montreal economy whose roots extended back to the years following World War I. The political concerns of English-speaking Montrealers would not have had the same result had it not been for the change in their economic prospects.

In their frequent unwillingness to recognize the economic bases for the problems they faced, English-speaking Montrealers of the 1970s shared much with Robert Sellar who in the first decade of the century wrote about the departure of English speakers from the Eastern Townships.[20] Sellar linked this population movement to various political decisions that seemed to encourage the movement of French speakers into this part of the province. This narrow focus blinded Sellar, however, from seeing the more basic economic motivation that was leading his English-speaking neighbours to abandon their farms for better lands in the prairies.

---

20. Sellar, *The Tragedy of Quebec*.

Sellar described the departure of English-speaking farmers as a tragedy, and to many English-speaking Montrealers who saw their families divided by the exodus of the 1970s something tragic had indeed taken place. There was probably little solace for these people in the fact that the departure of English-speaking Montrealers was only the most recent stage in a process that had begun in the mid-nineteenth century. Nevertheless, it is important to retain this historical perspective in order to understand the economic bases of the departures from Montreal during the 1970s.

SELECT BIBLIOGRAPHY

Boulet, Jac-André. *Language and Earnings in Montreal.* Ottawa, 1980.

Bradbury, Bettina. "The Family Economy and Work in an Industrializing City", CHA *Papers*, 1979, pp. 71-96.

Copp, Terry. *The Anatomy of Poverty.* Toronto, 1974.

Jocas, Yves de and Guy Rocher. "Inter-Generational Mobility in the Province of Quebec", *Canadian Journal of Economics and Political Science*, XXIII (1953), 57-68.

Lacroix, Robert et François Vaillancourt. *Les revenus et la langue au Québec.* Quebec, 1981.

Reynolds, Lloyd. *The British Immigrant.* Toronto, 1935.

IX

The Evolution
of English Education
in Quebec

As a result of the changes described in the previous three chapters, English-speaking Quebec was totally transformed in the post-Confederation period. No longer an overwhelmingly British population with strong roots in various parts of the province, English-speaking Quebec by the late twentieth century had become ethnically diverse and concentrated in Montreal, where a once powerful English-speaking elite had seen its influence greatly reduced. These changes were so profound that they fundamentally altered the way in which English-speaking Quebecers participated in the affairs of the province. This chapter examines the place of English speakers in the province's public school system, while the following chapter looks at the role of the linguistic minority in Quebec politics since Confederation. In both cases the primary goal is to employ aspects of institutional change to mirror the changes that English-speaking Quebec experienced between 1867 and 1980.

1. Establishing the Structures of English Education, 1867-1875

In the immediate aftermath of the Rebellion of 1837 a few Quebecers dreamed of a system of common schools in which all children in a given community, regardless of religion, would be educated together. By the mid-1840s, however, this notion was already dead as a school system was formed that had separate Catholic and Protestant structures in both Montreal and Quebec City and the potential for a similar division elsewhere. Outside the two major cities common schools could exist, but the local religious minority, be it Catholic or Protestant, could opt out and establish dissentient schools of its own. Accordingly, the religious polarization of Quebec society was already reflected in the structure of Quebec education well before Confederation had even been proposed. However, the beginnings of negotiations that would ultimately lead to Confederation pushed certain Protestants to demand a clearer definition of their educational rights. They saw the creation of the largely Catholic province of Quebec as a potential threat to their interests, particularly in the light of the aggressive Catholic revival then in progress under the leadership of Montreal's Bishop Bourget and Bishop Laflèche of Trois-Rivières. Lobbying by men such as Alexander Galt resulted in the incorporation of Article 93 into the BNA Act, which provided constitutional guarantees for those Protestant educational rights that were in existence as of 1 July 1867.

The inclusion of Article 93 was only a partial victory for men such as Galt. Given the wording of this clause, they wanted to extend the nature of Protestant rights prior to the introduction of Confederation. The Langevin Bill of 1866 was an effort in that direction, but it was never passed. Nevertheless, the efforts of Protestant leaders to extend their rights continued after the beginning of the new political regime, even though such concessions would not be constitutionally guaranteed by Article 93. Galt felt that the fight had to be continued in the face of the crusade being led by Bourget and Laflèche. He took the threat of Catholic aggression against Protestants so seriously that he wrote in the 1870s about the possible separation of the predominantly English enclaves from the province.[1] While such a political separation was impossible, a more limited separation was achieved in the educational sphere. It took the form of a radical transformation of the Council of Public Instruction.

The Council had been formed in 1856 to provide direction for the province's education system, which was at that time administered by an appointed superintendent. This structure provided the illusion of a unified system, since a single official received advice from a council of Catholics and Protestants who deliberated together. With the coming of Confederation the superintendent was replaced by a minister of public instruction, placing control over education in the hands of an elected official. However, the power of the minister was already under attack when the Educational Act was revised in 1869. This act divided the Council of Public Institution (CPI) into two separate committees, one Catholic and one Protestant, each of which was to deliberate over issues relevant to its jurisdiction. Since it had been decided to concentrate power in these denominational committees, the usefulness of a minister providing a single direction for Quebec education was reduced, and in 1875 the Ministry of Public Instruction was abolished, not to be resurrected until 1964. With the Ministry out of the way, the two committees were in a position to run Quebec education without political interference, and there were few people in either the Catholic or Protes-

1. Alexander Galt, *Civil Liberties in Quebec* (Montreal, 1876).

tant camps who were bothered by this change. For many Catholics, the suppression of the role of the State and the end of collaboration with the Protestants was welcomed. For Protestants who were suspicious of Catholicism, both in the guise of the Quebec government and in the form of bishops on the Catholic committee, the 1875 changes were similarly desirable. As an opponent of the 1875 revisions, Galt stood out as an exceptional figure.[2]

Quebec's system of denominational schools run by two denominational committees marked the period from 1875 to 1964. To the extent that the denominational nature of all Quebec schools was still in force at the start of the 1980s, many aspects of this system survived beyond the establishment of a Ministry of Education in 1964. This was a system that perpetuated a particular vision of Quebec based upon the values that were dominant in the mid-nineteenth century. For educational purposes, Quebecers, regardless of their mother tongue, were to be divided into Catholic and Protestant camps. In the late nineteenth century this created difficulties for English-speaking Catholics who did not quite fit into the structures that had been established. Into the twentieth century, the system had further difficulties in accommodating the various linguistic and religious groups that arrived in Quebec. Many of these groups came to form part of the English-speaking population, so that the problems faced by the Quebec educational system mirrored changes in the composition of English-speaking Quebec.

2. Mair, *Quest for Quality*, p. 24.

2. English-Catholic Education

G.W. Parmelee was asked to write the entry on English education in Quebec for the encyclopedic *Canada and its Provinces*, whose numerous volumes were published early in the 1900s.[3] Parmelee's piece, which was published in 1914, provided a striking example of an author straying from his assigned topic. From beginning to end Parmelee discussed Protestant education to the complete exclusion of English-Catholic education. This is hardly surprising given Parmelee's place within the Protestant educational structure. He served as the secretary of the Protestant committee of the CPI from 1891 to 1930. With this position he was the director of Protestant education in the province, a title which he received officially in 1925.[4] Like other Protestant leaders before him, Parmelee chose to forget that Protestant education was not synonymous with English education. As Table 9.1 indicates, at the time that Parmelee wrote his piece, nearly all students in the Protestant system were English-speaking. Nevertheless, of all English students over one-quarter were Catholic. The problem for these English Catholics was the denominational structure of Quebec education, which placed them in a system where they made up less than 5 % of all students. Protestant leaders simply turned a blind eye to these English speakers, assuming for themselves the right to speak for the educational concerns of English-speaking Quebec.

---

3. G.W. Parmelee, "English Education", in A. Shortt and A. Doughty, eds , *Canada and Its Provinces* (Toronto, 1914), XVI, pp. 445-501.
4. Mair, p. 24.

TABLE 9.1

Language and Religion
of Students in Quebec Schools, 1911

| | MOTHER TONGUE | | |
RELIGION	ENGLISH	FRENCH	TOTAL
Protestant	47,305	1,693	48,998
Catholic	17,028	341,828	358,856
Total	64,333	343,521	407,854

Source: *Annuaire du Québec* 1911-12; these figures include all students registered in elementary schools, model schools, and academies.

Largely abandoned by their Protestant co-linguists, the English-speaking Catholics were left to battle for better facilities on their own with a bureaucracy that was predominantly made up of French-speaking clerics. In Montreal this battle was largely fought by Irish Catholics whose children were educated by the Montreal Catholic School Commission (MCSC). Between 1860 and 1895 the MCSC was run by a six man board, three of whose members were appointed by the city of Montreal with the other three named by the provincial government. In such a system the Irish had to depend upon the goodwill of the French majority to gain membership on the board. Throughout the late 1800s the Irish usually had representation on the board of the MCSC, but this did not preclude complaints regarding the facilities provided for the English Catholics.[5] As Roger Magnuson has noted, "Irish Catholic children [in the nineteenth century] attended French schools in which English-language classes were set up... Owing to a lack of

_____
5. D.S. Cross, "The Irish in Montreal", p. 123.

English-language teachers, students were often taught in the English classes by French-Canadian teachers."[6] To make matters worse, the schools in the Irish districts were frequently described as being in a deplorable state. An 1884 provincial examination of the Montreal schools singled out St. Bridget's School for special attention because "the children who [attended] the school and the professors who [taught] in it... [did] so at the great peril of their health, if not at the risk of their lives."[7]

Whether the poorer members of the English-Catholic population received facilities from the MCSC that were any worse than those provided in French working class districts is difficult to determine. For English-speaking Catholics with the means to educate their children beyond the primary level, there were two private schools, Loyola College, established in 1896, and the Catholic High School of Montreal, which opened three years later.[8] By sending their children to private schools, the wealthier English-Catholic parents, like their French-speaking counterparts, lost any incentive to try to improve the public schools largely frequented by the poor. According to historian Terry Copp, all working class Catholics, regardless of language, had poor facilities. To him, "the real problem for Catholic education was its sharp division along class lines."[9]

That certain French-Catholic students were also suffering from inadequate facilities within the MCSC was probably of little comfort to English-Catholic leaders whose complaints transcended this particular issue. There was also the recurring complaint that they

6. *Ibid.*, p. 81.
7. *Ibid.*, p. 128.
8. Prior to 1896 private English-Catholic education was available at St. Mary's College (Collège Ste-Marie) where both French and English students were taught.
9. Copp, p. 69.

did not have either a curriculum or textbooks tailored to their particular needs. Up until the 1930s the English-Catholic schools employed translations of the materials used in the French schools. Not until the 1930s was there a teachers' training college in Montreal for English-speaking Catholics. Until 1938 the Catholic teachers' college in Montreal, the Jacques Cartier Normal School, operated in French, so that English Catholics "had to manage as best they could."[10]

The place of the English Catholics within the Catholic educational structure began to change, however, with the establishment in 1928 of a semi-autonomous committee within the MCSC to supervise English language education. Then, during the 1930s and 1940s there were a number of reforms that created a separate English-Catholic curriculum along with separate examinations and textbooks.[11] By the 1940s the English Catholics had achieved a certain autonomy within the MCSC and had secured structures that made their system appear very similar to that enjoyed by the city's English-speaking Protestants. For instance, the public high school was a feature of the Protestant educational system. The establishment in 1931 of D'Arcy McGee, the first public English-Catholic high school, was therefore a sign that language was becoming more important than religion in influencing the structure of English-Catholic education.[12]

English Catholics had long demanded institutions that reflected their particular interests. For instance, they sought exams for their students that would allow them to enter Montreal's only English-language uni-

---

10. Mair, p. 21.

11. G. Emmett Carter, *The Catholic Public Schools of Quebec* (Toronto, 1957).

12. T.W.R. Wilson, "A History of the English-Catholic Public Schools of Quebec", Report Prepared for the Royal Commission on Bilingualism and Biculturalism, 1965.

versity, McGill. But why did the French-speaking clerical leaders of the MCSC finally give in to these demands beginning in the late 1920s? At least part of the
answer is to be found in the changing composition of
Montreal's Catholic population. The early years of the
twentieth century had seen the arrival, for the first
time in Quebec's history, of large numbers of immigrants who had neither French nor English as their
mother tongue. The largest group among these immigrants was the Jews who provided a particular challenge to the province's educational system, for they
had neither English nor French as their mother tongue,
and were neither Catholic nor Protestant. The problems of integrating them into the structures that had
been put in place by 1875 will be discussed in the next
section of this chapter.

   In addition to the Jews, there were also several
groups that had come to Quebec by the 1930s with
neither French nor English as their mother tongue, but
with Catholicism as their religion. The most important
of these were the Italians who numbered nearly 25,000
in 1931. The arrival of these new Catholics created a
dilemma for the French-speaking clerics who ran the
Catholic schools. Until this time, the only non-French
speakers in the Catholic system had been the British
origin Catholics, who naturally gravitated to the English schools. Now, however, there was the problem
of how to deal with these non-British Catholic students
who already numbered over 7,000 within the MCSC in
1931, as opposed to fewer than 10,000 British origin
students. [13] If these new students were to be permitted
to enter the French system in large numbers then the
traditional role of the French-Catholic school as a place
where certain values could be transmitted to a
homogeneous student body would be destroyed.

---

13. MCSC Archives, Relevé des nationalités pour le mois de septembre
    1931.

TABLE 9.2

Ethnicity of Students in English Sector of MCSC,
1931-1960

ETHNIC ORIGIN	1931	1960
French	1,957 (13 %)	4,400 (16 %)
British	8,797 (59 %)	9,394 (34 %)
Italian	1,666 (11 %)	8,510 (30 %)
Others	2,419 (16 %)	5,669 (20 %)
Total	14,839	27,937

Source: MCSC Archives, Relevé des nationalités pour le mois de septembre 1931; mai 1960.

That the Italians and other newcomers might pose
a threat appeared clear to certain clerics from the fact
that 63 % of all Italian origin students were attending
French schools in 1931. Rather than have to deal with
such students in the French schools, these French-
Catholic leaders encouraged the establishment of a
semi-autonomous English sector which would be provided with the means to educate all Catholics whose
mother tongue was not French. As political scientist
Henry Milner has noted, the Catholic hierarchy encouraged "la création d'un secteur catholique auto-
nome de langue anglaise pour accueillir non seulement
les Irlandais mais bientôt nombre de catholiques non-
francophones qui auraient autrement fréquenté les
écoles de langue française. Les élites du début du XXᵉ
siècle, héritières spirituelles des catholiques ultramon-
tains du siècle précédent, entretenaient des convictions
nationalistes conservatrices. Elles estimaient que la
survivance des Canadiens-français reposait sur leur
langue et sur leur religion et sur les institutions qui les
maintenaient."[14]

---

14. Henry Milner, *La réforme scolaire au Québec* (Montreal, 1984), p. 33.

As the above table indicates, students who were of neither French nor British origin already constituted over one-quarter of the student population in the English schools of the MCSC in 1931. In the decades that followed, the attitude of the French-Catholic leaders, together with the autonomy of the English sector, allowed this figure to grow until half of the student body in the English schools by 1960 was of neither French nor British origin. In 1960 the Italians alone were nearly as numerous within the English-Catholic schools as were students of British origin. By 1977 nearly half of all students in the English sector of the MCSC were of Italian origin.[15] This was a reflection of the steady routing of Italian students into the English stream, particularly in the post World War II era. While the majority of Italian students were enrolled in the French schools of the MCSC in 1943, this figure dwindled to 28 % by 1960 and to 10 % by 1973.[16]

The process by which the Italians and other newcomers to Quebec were integrated into the English schools of the MCSC was the result of a number of factors. The structure of the Montreal economy encouraged immigrants to demand an English education for their children. This trend was supported by the unwillingness of the French schools to receive these new Quebecers. As for the English sector, its administrators used their autonomy to assure themselves that subsequent generations of Italians would continue to frequent their schools. In the 1950s there were various proposals to provide Italian students in the English sector with a solid grounding in both French and

15. Donat Taddeo and Raymond Taras, "The Language of Education Debate: A Study of the Political Dynamics Between Quebec's Educational Authorities and the Italian Community", unpublished manuscript, p. 190. I am most grateful to Donat Taddeo for putting this manuscript, unpublished at the moment this book was prepared, at my disposal.

16. *Ibid.*, p. 78.

English. Such proposals would have provided these students with the means to integrate more easily into French-speaking society. If this had occurred, then the children of the next generation might have opted for French schools. Accordingly, when English-Catholic leaders on the board of the MCSC blocked these proposals they were looking out for the preservation of their clientele. [17]

This routing of the children of post-World War II immigrants into the English sector of the MCSC had several clear implications. First, it provided the means whereby nearly half of all students in English schools in the province were in Catholic institutions by 1980. As Table 9.3 indicates, only 30 % of the province's English school population was in Catholic schools in 1901, a figure that gradually fell until the end of World War II and the arrival of the new immigrants. For the island of Montreal, by the mid-1970s a majority of the students in English schools were enrolled in the various Catholic boards. [18]

The English-Catholic school became the vehicle by which the children of post-World War II immigrants to Quebec gained a firm knowledge of English. These students then frequently passed English along as the mother tongue of their own children, thus fuelling the fears of certain French speakers by the 1960s. As the birth rate among French speakers plummeted, the channeling of immigrants into the English stream came to be perceived by some as a threat. The earlier belief that the French-Catholic population could best be protected by its isolation from "foreign" elements was thus replaced by the need to integrate those very

---

17. *Ibid.*, p. 117.
18. Lise Bissonnette, "School Restructuration on the Island of Montreal: A Missed Opportunity for Anglophones", in Caldwell and Waddell, eds., *The English of Quebec*, p. 285.

TABLE 9.3

Percentage of Students in Quebec's English Language Schools
Enrolled in Catholic Institutions,
1901-1980

YEAR	PERCENT
1901	30.4
1911	26.4
1918	24.6
1929	23.4
1940	23.2
1950	23.0
1959	34.4
1960	37.5
1970	45.5
1980	45.6

Source: *Report of the Superintendent of Public Instruction*, 1901-1960; Ministère de l'Éducation, *La Clientèle Scolaire*, 1970-80.

elements into French-speaking society. In the face of predictions that French speakers might make up less than half of the population of metropolitan Montreal by the year 2000, efforts were made to restrict access to English schools for the children of immigrants who had neither French nor English as their mother tongue.[19] This new attitude gained public exposure in the St-Léonard school crisis of 1968, in which the local Catholic school board attempted to deny English education to the area's primarily Italian children. In the 1970s this restrictive approach took the form of legislation with the passage of Bill 22 in 1974 and Bill 101 in 1977, both of which sought to limit access to English schools.

19. Henripin, "Quebec and the Demographic Dilemma".

Faced with a clear challenge to the well-being of the English-Catholic sector, its leaders looked to their Protestant counterparts for support. Some sympathy was found, particularly on the issue of admission to English schools, since the Protestant schools also stood to be affected by the language legislation, although to a lesser extent than the English-Catholic schools. By the mid-1970s some English-Catholic leaders were looking for more than sympathy from the English-speaking Protestants, as they began to accept the idea of school boards structured along linguisitic lines.[20] On the surface it would appear that this was an idea whose time had come. There was little difference in the curriculum of the English-Catholic and English-Protestant schools, and the two had roughly equal numbers of students. Nevertheless, there was little support from Protestant educational leaders for such a reorganization. From their point of view, the abandoning of boards based upon religion threatened the guarantees for denominational schools in Article 93 of the BNA Act. They feared that once Protestant boards were gone the provincial government would be free to do what it pleased with the running of all the province's English schools. So, a structure that poorly reflected the diversity of the English-speaking population in the 1860s still existed at the start of the 1980s, in spite of the profound demographic changes that had taken place within that population.

---

20. Bissonnette, p. 287.

3. Protestant Education and the Ethnic Transformation of English-Speaking Quebec

When Protestant leaders fought for the inclusion of Article 93 in the BNA Act, they were fighting to defend the schools of a minority which was solidly British; there were few students in the Protestant schools of 1867 who could not trace their roots back to England, Scotland or Ireland. In 1891 the homogeneity of the students in the province's Protestant schools was reflected in the fact that 94 % had English as their mother tongue. A further 5 % were French speakers, while only 1 % had neither French nor English as their mother tongue. By 1980 the percentage of English mother tongue students in the Protestant schools had fallen to 78 %, largely because of the increase to 15 % of the portion of the student body which had neither French nor English as its mother tongue.[21] The children of recent immigrants were making up an ever-growing percentage of the student population of the Protestant schools, taking over some of the desks left empty by students of British origin whose parents had left Quebec in large numbers beginning in the mid-1960s. As a result of their dependence upon immigrant children, Protestant educators joined English-Catholic leaders in calling for easy access to English language schools in the face of the language legislation of the 1970s.

The English-Catholic and English-Protestant systems differed, however, in the fact that the former only really felt the full impact of immigrant children in the post-World War II era, while the Protestant schools played the major role in educating the children of immigrants who had come to Quebec prior to the Great Depression. Jews made up the single most important group of Quebecers who came to the province

---

21. Report of the Superintendent of Public Instruction, 1891-2; Ministère de l'Éducation, *La Clientèle Scolaire*, 1980-1.

prior to the 1930s with neither French nor English as their mother tongue. Their situation was further complicated, however, by the fact that they did not neatly fit into an educational system that was polarized along Catholic-Protestant lines. In the late nineteenth century, when the Jewish population was relatively small, most Jewish parents sought to send their children to Protestant schools. They wanted an English education for their children and were put off by the more explicit religious content of the Catholic curriculum. Nevertheless, from time to time wealthier Jewish parents worked out arrangements with the MCSC whereby they would pay their school taxes to the Catholic board in return for the establishment of schools of their own where the normal curriculum of the MCSC would not be used. As for the poorer elements in the Jewish population, they continued to send their children to the Protestant schools.

This was the situation that existed in 1903 when the Quebec legislature passed an act to clarify the status of the Jews with regard to education. The Protestant leaders wanted to secure the Jewish tax dollars that were being lost to the MCSC. Accordingly, the 1903 act recognized Jews as Protestants for educational purposes so that both Jewish tax dollars and Jewish students would go to the Protestant schools. The 1903 deal appeared to settle the issue, but it could not take into account the massive immigration of relatively poor, non-tax paying Jews that was just beginning. The Protestant leaders had shown themselves to be more interested in Jewish tax dollars than in the education of the Jewish children. Now it began to appear that the Jews were a strain on Protestant school finances. By the early 1920s Jewish children made up nearly 40 % of the students in Montreal's Protestant schools and were widely described as "our educational problem" by Protestant officials who saw too many Jewish students with too little Jewish tax revenue to pay for their education. [22] In a system that was defined along Catholic-Protestant lines, why should Protestants have to pay for the education of these non-Protestants? Such questions were no doubt encouraged by the increasingly frequent demands of Jewish leaders for the right to representation on the Protestant school board and for the hiring of more Jewish teachers. These demands coupled with the financial issue ultimately sent the question of the Jewish presence in the Protestant schools to the courts for clarification.

In a series of court decisions ending with that by the Judicial Committee of the Privy Council in 1928, the 1903 law was found ultra vires, or unconstitutional. It was found that by giving Jews the same status as Protestants the 1903 law violated Article 93 of the BNA Act, which was explicit in only specifying rights for Catholics and Protestants. A new agreement then had to be found. In 1930 the provincial government granted additional funds to the Protestant boards to silence their complaints about the cost of educating Jewish students. The Jews were to have access to the Protestant schools, but no arrangement was made for the appointment of Jewish school commissioners, a situation that did not change until 1965.

From the 1930s on Jewish parents sent their children to the Protestant schools where they acquired an ability to function in English. When they grew older, these students passed English along as the mother tongue of their own children. Accordingly, the Protestant schools served as the vehicle for the integration of the Jews into English-speaking Quebec. However, given the religious prejudices that existed well into the twentieth century, this process did not take place smoothly. Since the structures of education in Quebec

22. E.I. Rexford, *Our Educational Problem: The Jewish Population and the Protestant Schools* (Montreal, 1924).

Bishop's University, 1949 (D.C. Masters, *Bishop's University: The First Hundred Years*).

McGill University
(Archives de la
Ville de Montréal)

were defined along confessional lines, certain Protestant leaders employed Article 93 to veil their antisemitism. Constitutional niceties could not be used, however, to limit the entrance of Jews to McGill University, an institution directed by English-Protestant leaders. Accordingly, McGill established quotas for the number of Jews who could be accepted. No constitutional issue could be raised in the McGill case, but the Jewish presence in the public schools demonstrated once again the inability of the educational structures established in the nineteenth century to cope with the more diverse Quebec population of the twentieth century.

4. Protestant Education and English Speakers Outside Montreal

For English-speaking Catholics seeking unified linguistic boards and for Jews seeking equal rights, the great stumbling block was Article 93 of the BNA Act, which could not respond to the ethnic diversity of twentieth century English-speaking Quebec. However, educational problems were also experienced during the twentieth century by another group within the linguistic minority, namely those living outside of Montreal. As was shown in Chapter VII, in most regions of Quebec other than the Montreal metropolitan area, the post-Confederation period was not kind to English speakers. With the decline of their numbers came a corresponding decline in influence within the educational structure that English speakers controlled, the Protestant system. Article 93 had nothing to do with the decline of services for these "off island" English speakers. This was simply a case of declining influence during a period of declining numbers.

Nowhere was the deterioration in Protestant education clearer than in the Eastern Townships. As a reflection of the strength of the English-speaking population of this region by the time of Confederation, the Townships possessed a complete range of Protestant educational facilities. Not only did the region boast numerous primary schools, but it also had many superior schools, model schools and academies, where students could further their education. To top off this system, of course, was Bishop's University at Lennoxville. In the half century following Confederation, however, the English-speaking population of the region declined, resulting in a loss of students, political power, and the ability to maintain the school system that had existed in 1867.

The decline of the rural English-speaking population of the region was well reflected, for instance, in the deterioration of the area's elementary schools. In his book, *The Tragedy of Quebec*, Robert Sellar reported the sad state of 835 rural Protestant schools, 100 of which "did not open from an inability to get a teacher for the salary the retepayers were able to offer; 200 [of wich] were kept open with difficulty, having only from five to eight students, and 300 [of wich] had less than a dozen."[23] As was usually the case, Sellar blamed the Catholic church for the plight of the schools. By establishing their own schools in the region, the clergy set up a situation in which local tax dollars were divided between two systems, neither of which could offer a sound education. In his typically ethnocentric fashion, Sellar noted that while the Catholics might have accepted such an education Protestants would not, thus further encouraging their departure from rural Quebec.

In most cases Sellar's analysis of the problems of rural Quebec rarely went beyond his anti-Catholicism. In this case, however, Sellar also noted the complicity of the members of the Protestant committee of the CPI

---

23. Sellar, p. 210.

who "for decades seemed to regard their main function as that of getting the largest possible share of the
education fund for their pet institutions."[24] As a consequence, the rural schools were hard pressed for funds,
a situation made worse when in 1897 the Protestant
committee ordered that only McGill-trained teachers
could be employed. Heretofore, teachers commanding
lower salaries and trained in local academies had staffed
the rural schools, but now, because of what Sellar
called the "McGill faction" on the Protestant committee, more costly teachers had to be employed.[25] The
cavalier attitude of Protestant educational officials was
similarly expressed in 1900 when a small sum of money was to be diverted from the two "Protestant" universities to support the rural schools. The chairman of
the Protestant committee balked, noting that "no one
is able to object to the aiding of the poor municipalities... However, the word poor is not restricted to
these municipalities when it is a question of education.
It also applies to the universities."[26] Rather than provide additional funds for rural schools, the Protestant
committee consistently supported a policy of con-
solidating those schools that still existed, thus encouraging the further departure of English speakers
who viewed the school as a central institution of their
community.[27]

The urban leaders on the Protestant committee
were no more forthcoming in their support for the
well-being of the academies and model schools of the

---

24. Robert Hill, "Robert Sellar and the Huntingdon Gleaner: The Con-
    science of Rural Protestant Quebec, 1863-1919", Ph.D. Thesis, McGill
    University, 1970, p. 677.
25. *Ibid.*, p. 681.
26. *Quebec Sessional Papers*, 1900, No. 101, Heneker to Lieutenant Gover-
    nor (my translation).
27. John Adams, *The Protestant Schools in the Province of Quebec* (London,
    1902); W.A.F. Hepburn, *Report of the Quebec Protestant Education
    Survey* (Quebec, 1938).

Townships. Historian Anne Drummond has linked the problems of these institutions between 1895 and 1915 to certain policies formulated by the committee. It was decided that grants would be withheld from the academies unless they employed specified textbooks and hired highly trained teachers. The costs incurred in introducing these so-called improvements often exceeded the grants that would have been withheld. Accordingly, some academies were forced to close, while others ended up with a curriculum that was ill-suited to the needs of rural students. As Drummond has noted, "[This] program of studies prepared rural pupils not to remain but to leave, to fit into an urban society."[28]

The anger of rural English speakers over their treatment at the hands of the Protestant committee was so great that they provided considerable support in 1897 and 1898 for the Marchand government's proposal to set up a State-run Ministry of Education. While people such as Robert Sellar had been traditionally sceptical of the Quebec government, in this case they were prepared to accept open political control over education in place of the operations of the Protestant committee which were carried on behind closed doors. In his newspaper, the *Huntingdon Gleaner*, Sellar welcomed the removal of power from men "who [applied] public funds in the building of a privileged interest."[29] One of Sellar's allies in the legislature was H.T. Duffy, the member for Brome. Duffy resented the elite which had run Protestant education. He noted that the CPI "n'[avait] pas de contact avec la population et c'[était] pour cette raison qu'il

---

28. Anne Drummond, "Rural Depopulation, Teacher Certification and the Course of Study in Quebec Protestant Superior Schools, 1885-1915," Paper presented to the Canadian History of Education Association, 1982, p. 21.
29. *Huntingdon Gleaner*, 6 January 1898.

n'[appuyait] pas le bill."[30] This elite did not have the power to block the bill in the legislative assembly, but the job was done instead in the legislative council. Reflecting the views of the English-speaking elite, the *Montreal Gazette* welcomed the council's actions which "respected the privileges of the minority."[31] Those such as Sellar and Duffy who wanted the State to intervene to distribute educational funds more equitably would have to wait until the 1960s.[32]

5. State Control and English Education

Those English-speaking Protestants who, in 1897-1898, supported the bill to give the state control over education were challenging the arrangement that had been agreed upon by the French-Catholic and English-Protestant elites in the first decade after Confederation. Both elites believed themselves well served by their autonomy. The French-Catholic clergy secured the ability to transmit certain cultural values without the intrusion of politicians. The English-Protestant elite assured itself that its wealth would be employed for Protestant education without the State intervening to distribute resources more equitably. Support for this arrangement was so strong that State control of education did not take place until the 1960s.

The impetus for this change came from French-speaking Quebec, which by the start of the 1960s had undergone some radical social changes. By that time a coalition of lay leaders had emerged to challenge the power of the church and of political leaders who believed that the government that governs least governs best. In the election of 1960 the Union Nationale was pushed aside, and the Liberals came into power

---

30. *Débats de l'assemblée législative du Québec*, 4 janvier 1898.
31. *Montreal Gazette*, 12 January 1898.
32. Drummond, p. 13.

committed to the active intervention of the State in the social and economic spheres. Within a few short years a "Quiet Revolution" occurred, as the Quebec government nationalized hydroelectric power, established its own pension plan, and took direct control over education. [33]

This last reform was, not surprisingly, greeted with little enthusiasm by the two elites that had long controlled Quebec education. In the case of the Protestants there was certainly evidence of opposition to the establishment of a Ministry of Education. For instance, in the election of 1960 the chairman of the province's most important Protestant school board, the Protestant School Board of Greater Montreal (PSBGM), supported the Union Nationale because of the Liberals' commitments to action in the field of education. [34] Similarly, when the Lesage government appointed a royal commission headed by Msgr. Alphonse-Marie Parent to pave the way for fundamental changes in the structure of education, briefs were submitted by two of the school boards on the island of Montreal. In its brief, the PSBGM expressed its resentment towards the notion that its constituents might have to pay provincial taxes to support boards which had not made a satisfactory effort to raise local taxes. [35] As for the Protestant School Commissioners of Pointe-Claire and Beaconsfield, they feared that State control might violate the principle that local property tax revenues should be used for local purposes. They demanded that "local school boards retain the right to impose property taxes

---

33. For further detail on this subject, see Kenneth McRoberts and Dale Posgate, *Quebec: Social Change and Political Crisis* (Toronto, 1980).
34. Jack Jedwab, "Montreal Anglophones and the Quiet Revolution", Paper presented to Canadian Political Science Association, 1984.
35. Protestant School Board of Greater Montreal, Brief (No. 170) to the Royal Commission of Inquiry on Education in Quebec (hereafter Parent Commission).

and [that] all such taxes should remain in the community where they [were] collected."[36]

The members of these two school boards were among the elite of Montreal's Protestant population. They recognized that the balance of political power in Quebec had shifted to such a degree that they could not really hope to block the State control of education. Just as the church had lost power within French-speaking Quebec to the new lay elite, so too had the English-speaking businessmen lost the economic clout that they had held earlier in the century. Nevertheless, these school commissioners still fought as best they could to retain the wealth of the Protestant population for the Protestant schools. Up until the 1960s the bulk of school revenues came from property taxes. In Montreal, Protestants paid their taxes for the support of Protestant schools, while Catholic taxes went to support Catholic schools. Taxes raised from corporations were divided between the two systems on the basis of the student population in each. In 1888, for instance, the greater wealth of certain English-speaking Protestants provided the Protestant Board of School Commissions with $16 per student, while the MCSC collected only $9. In spite of this unequal level of funding there were Protestant leaders in the 1880s who sought a widening of the disparities by assigning the taxes paid by Protestant-run corporations to the Protestant schools.[37] As Robert Sellar would later ask, "Is a man less of a Protestant because of his having incorporated his business?"[38]

By asking that locally raised funds be made available for local schools and that all boards make an equal

---

36. Protestant School Commissioners of Pointe-Claire and Beaconsfield, Brief (No. 185) to the Parent Commission, n.p.

37. Louis-Philippe Audet, *Histoire du Conseil de l'instruction publique* (Montreal, 1964), pp. 110-114; 251-256.

38. Sellar, p. 213.

effort to support their schools, the Protestant school commissioners of the early 1960s followed in Sellar's footsteps. Between 1956 and 1965 the share of total school revenues derived from local property taxes declined from 55 % to 43 %, while provincial contributions increased from 29 % to 52 %. The Protestant boards were powerless to stop this change in the financing of Quebec education. What they had requested was that certain assurances be provided that no wholesale shifting of funds from wealthy Protestant boards to less well endowed boards would take place. This principle was endorsed in the report of the Parent commission.[39] Ultimately, however, such recommendations did not have the force of constitutional guarantees. The Protestant boards only had such guarantees for the rights that they possessed as of 1 July 1867. If a provincial ministry of education chose to use its financial power to equalize the resources of Quebec's school boards, there was little that the Protestant leaders could do. Similarly, they were impotent when it came to government restrictions on access to English-language schools for certain categories of students. Once the State chose to assume control over education, it meant the end of the autonomy previously enjoyed by the Catholic and Protestant elites.

5. Conclusion

Although the State took control of education in the 1960s, at the start of the 1980s the denominational structure of Quebec's schools still existed. This structure had been given constitutional support in Article 93 of the BNA Act and was reinforced in the first years after Confederation. By 1875 certain Protestant leaders had used their economic influence to secure control over the Protestant schools which then were educating

---

39. Quebec, *Report of the Commission of Inquiry on Education in the Province of Quebec* (Quebec, 1966), V.

the vast majority of English-speaking students. In the Protestant schools nearly all the students were of British origin. In the century that followed, however, the composition of the English-speaking population was transformed, creating difficulties for the structures established under the circumstances of 1875. The decline in the influence of Montreal's business elite played a role in the loss of the autonomy long wielded by the Protestant committee of the CPI. The Protestant system also had to adjust to the arrival of the Jews, whose presence was not accounted for in the original structure of Quebec education. The elites of the 1870s could not have imagined a day when the number of students in the English-Catholic system would equal that in the English-Protestant schools. This last development created pressure for the restructuring of Quebec's educational system along linguistic lines, but at the start of the 1980s Article 93 remained to block this fundamental change in the structures that had been put in place over a century earlier.

SELECT BIBLIOGRAPHY

Audet, Louis-Philippe. *Histoire de l'enseignement au Québec*. Montreal, 1971.

Bissonnette, Lise. "School Restructuration on the Island of Montreal: A Missed Opportunity for Anglophones," in Caldwell and Waddell, *English of Quebec*, pp. 279-92.

Magnuson, Roger. *A Brief History of Quebec Education*. Montreal, 1980.

Mair, Nathan. *The Quest for Quality in the Protestant Public Schools of Quebec*. Quebec, 1980.

Sellar, Robert. *The Tragedy of Quebec*. Toronto, 1974.

X

English-Speaking Quebec and Post-Confederation Politics

Quebecers went to the polls to register their preferences regarding provincial matters three times between 1976 and 1981. Upon each of these occasions there was a considerable difference between the behaviour of English-speaking and French-speaking Quebecers. In the provincial elections of 1976 and 1981 Parti québécois governments came into power without a single PQ member being elected in any of the predominantly English ridings in the province. Similarly, the 1980 referendum on sovereignty-association indicated a parting of the ways of the two linguistic groupings. Roughly half of all French speakers voted "yes" in the referendum, and the fifteen ridings which gave majorities to the "yes" option were all predominantly French-speaking ridings. By contrast, the strongest opposition to the concept of sovereignty-association came from ridings largely populated by English speakers. Leading the way was the Montreal riding of D'Arcy McGee in which 96 % of the voters voted "no".

Because English-speaking Quebecers found themselves in an isolated position within Quebec politics by the late 1970s, it was tempting for some observers to

assume that the linguistic minority had always occupied such a marginal position. The Montreal Island
School Council, for example, noted in a 1983 pamphlet, "La population anglaise s'était depuis long-
temps désintéressée de la vie des organismes
nationaux du Québec: vie parlementaire, vie munici-
pale et fonction publique."[1] The council's goal in pub-
lishing this pamphlet was to make students aware of
the diversity within the population of Montreal. Instead, however, it provided a caricature of the English-
speaking population by assuming that the situation
that existed at the time of the pamphlet's publication
was the same as that which had existed over a long
stretch of Quebec history. Moreover, it discussed only
the position of English speakers in provincial politics
and made no effort to see whether the linguistic minority had behaved in a distinctive manner on the
federal level.

In order to provide a fuller description of the role
of English-speaking Quebecers in both provincial and
federal politics, this chapter will examine two different
types of issues. First, the behaviour of English speakers at the polls will be analyzed in order to see
whether the linguistic minority voted in a fashion that
was distinctive from the majority over the period from
1867 to 1980. Following this analysis of electoral behaviour there will be a discussion of the role of English
speakers in defining the political ground rules under
which all elected officials perform. Some of these rules
are explicit and can be found in the BNA Act; others
are unwritten and govern such issues as cabinet formation. Both types of rules changed over time, and the
ability of the English-speaking population to have its
interests recognized reflected the power it wielded at
any given moment. In a similar vein, how English

---

1. Conseil Scolaire de l'Ile de Montréal, *Les Anglais* (Montreal, 1983),
n.p.

speakers voted reflected certain aspects of the changing composition of that population. In examining the political history of English Quebec from 1867 to 1980, this chapter will use the political system as a further means of highlighting the changes which the English-speaking population experienced in the post-Confederation period.

1. English-Speaking Quebec at the Polls

In the 1980 referendum on sovereignty-association the English-speaking minority voted overwhelmingly "no" while the French majority was evenly split between the two options. There were other moments in Quebec's past, however, when the divisions between the two groups were even more pronounced. Such was the case, for instance, in 1942 when the federal government held a plebiscite to ask the Canadian voters to free it of the promise it had made at the start of World War II never to use conscripted soldiers for overseas duty. This promise had been made to French Canadians, and more particularly to French-speaking Quebecers, who had shown their disdain for conscription in World War I. French speakers did not appreciate the fact that the government of Mackenzie King was asking all Canadians to free it of a promise made exclusively to them. Not surprisingly, the French vote in the plebiscite was overwhelmingly negative, reaching 98 % in the riding of Beauce. There were only nine ridings in the province that agreed to free the King government of its promise, and these were all ridings in Montreal where the English-speaking population was large. For instance, the voters of the predominantly English riding of St-Antoine-Westmount gave 85 % of their votes to the "yes" side.

The problem that both the federal plebiscite of 1942 and the provincial referendum of 1980 pose for the historian is to know whether they were representative of a regular parting of the ways at the polls of Quebec's two major linguistic groupings. As a first step towards answering this question, the two subsections that follow will be based largely upon an analysis of every election, both provincial and federal, between 1867 and 1980, focusing upon the victorious party in each riding in each election. Whether predominantly English ridings consistently sided with a different party from that preferred in French-speaking ridings will be determined after defining English ridings as ones where the majority of the population had English as its mother tongue. To be certain that English-French differences are not confused with urban-rural differences, the party preferences of Montreal ridings will be compared with the choices of ridings situated elsewhere in the province.[2]

a) *English Speakers and Provincial Elections*

In August and September of 1867 Quebecers went to the polls to elect members to both the new Canadian Parliament and the new Quebec legislative assembly. As far as most English speakers were concerned, the latter election was the more novel of the two as they had been voting for years for their representatives to the legislature of the united Canadas. The Canadian

2. This system of assessing the voting behaviour of English Quebecers is not without its problems. Ideally, such an analysis would look at the distribution of the vote in each polling district and not merely the victorious party in each riding. It would then be possible to correlate the percentage of the population that was English with the distribution of the vote. To refine this procedure even further, urban-rural differences would have to be defined in a more sophisticated manner than simply differentiating Montreal from the rest of the province. Such an analysis would be incredibly time-consuming and, accordingly, could not be carried out for the purposes of this book.

Parliament was seen as much the same body with Maritime representatives included. By contrast, the existence of a separate legislature for Quebec was something new, and to many English speakers it was no doubt something to be feared. Would the French majority use the province's control over certain jurisdictions to make life difficult for English speakers? This type of question must have been in the minds of a number of English speakers as they made their way to vote in the first provincial election. Perhaps this uncertainty was the cause for the unanimity among English speakers in 1867 as all ten English ridings returned Conservative members. In the other ridings in the province, 41 seats went to the Conservatives and thirteen went to the Liberals.

When the first English-speaking members headed off to sit in the Quebec legislature, they gave some thought to sitting together, apart from the French-speaking Conservatives. Once in the assembly, however, they realized that their concerns were very similar to those of their French counterparts, as all members were interested in advancing the interests of the area they were representing. The English-speaking members slowly came to see themselves as representatives of certain parts of Quebec and not as representatives of English-speaking interests, a transformation that earned them the disapproval of several English newspapers.[3]

The residents of the largely English-speaking ridings also underwent a change in orientation following the first days of Confederation. Like their members,

---

3. Pierre Corbeil, "Les députés anglophones et le premier gouvernement du Québec de 1867 à 1871", Ph.D. Thesis, Université de Montréal, 1978, p. 236. Regarding the same period, also see Brendan O'Donnell, "Consociationalism, English Quebec and the Chauveau Ministry, 1867-72: A Study of Political Accommodation", M.A. Thesis, Wilfrid Laurier University, 1980.

the voters came to realize that the Quebec government was not going to oppress them, so they were able to look seriously at both the Conservative and Liberal parties, in spite of the latter's reputation as the more ardent defender of French-speaking interests. As Table 10.1 indicates, English speakers supported the Liberals far less frequently than did French speakers between 1867 and 1892, a period during which the Tories generally held power in the province.[4] Nevertheless, on the Island of Montreal English speakers were actually more supportive of the Liberals than were their French counterparts. English-speaking Montreal's support for the Liberals was even evident in the election of 1886 in which the Liberals of Honoré Mercier swept into power upon an explicitly nationalistic platform in the aftermath of the execution of Louis Riel.[5] Historian H.B. Neatby has asserted that "in the provincial election of 1886 no English Liberal was elected in either the Eastern Townships or Montreal. Not until 1888 was Mercier able to secure a seat in the assembly for an English Liberal to whom he could give a portfolio."[6] In fact, the two English Montreal ridings were divided between the Liberals and Conservatives, with the Montreal-Cartier seat going to James McShane, who served in Mercier's first cabinet as Minister of Agriculture and Public Works.

---

4. The Liberal party is being used as the basis for analysis as it existed as a functioning organization throughout the period under study. By contrast, the provincial Conservative party passed from the scene in the 1930s.

5. The party led by Mercier was officially known as the Parti National, but for all intents and purposes it was the Liberal party under another label.

6. H.B. Neatby, *Laurier and a Liberal Quebec* (Toronto, 1973), pp. 31-32.

TABLE 10.1

Quebec Provincial Elections,
1867-1976

| | % OF SEATS WON BY LIBERALS | | | |
	1867-92	1897-1935	1935-56	1960-76
Quebec	37	81	31	58
French	39	81	29	56
English	23	76	64	85
Montreal	26	63	56	69
French	15	68	47	62
English	40	59	76	96
Rest of Province	40	83	27	57
French	43	83	27	57
English	18	95	33	75

Source: Québec, Bibliothèque de la Législature, *Répertoire des parlementaires québécois, 1867-1978* (Quebec, 1980).

While English speakers in Montreal were more favourably inclined towards the Liberals than French speakers in the city between 1867 and 1892, the opposite situation existed off the island, thereby destroying any neat division of political behaviour along linguistic lines. According to Jean Hamelin, Jacques Letarte and Marcel Hamelin, rural English support for the Conservatives was a form of "gratitude d'un groupe minoritaire envers le parti qui, par la Confédération... lui a garanti l'exercice de ses droits les plus chers."[7] In particular, rural English speakers had cause to thank the Conservatives for the inclusion of Article 80 in the BNA Act by which their representation in the Quebec

---

7. Jean Hamelin, Jacques Letarte et Marcel Hamelin, "Les élections provinciales dans le Québec", *Cahiers de géographie du Québec* (1959-60), p. 190.

legislative assembly appeared to be guaranteed. As will be seen in the last section of this chapter, this guarantee proved useless in the face of the linguistic transformation of regions such as the Eastern Townships. Nevertheless, the appearance of a guarantee was sufficient to cause rural English speakers to vote differently from their counterparts in Montreal.

Rural-urban differences clouded the linguistic divisions evident between 1867 and 1892, and a similar situation also existed in the second period to be discussed. In the first period the Conservatives dominated Quebec politics, while between 1897 and 1935 the Liberals held uninterrupted control of the Quebec government. During these years of Liberal dominance, English and French ridings returned roughly the same percentage of Liberal members. For both groups, however, Liberal support was greater outside Montreal than it was in the city. To further complicate the picture, English Quebecers outside Montreal more frequently returned Liberal members than did their French counterparts, while in the city the French ridings were more likely to elect Liberals. There was no clear difference in the behaviour of English and French speakers in the general shift of the political preference of all Quebecers towards the Liberals. Interestingly, rural English speakers who were the most devoted supporters of the Conservatives between 1867 and 1892, became the most avid Liberals between 1897 and 1935. Perhaps these English speakers were expressing their insecurity by sticking close to the party in power.

Between 1936 and 1956 all but one provincial election was won by the Union Nationale (UN) headed by Maurice Duplessis. During these years rural English speakers continued to demonstrate their willingness to back the winner as they strongly supported the Union Nationale. These English speakers were also representative of the generally higher level of support for the Union Nationale among all rural Quebecers than existed in Montreal. In the city, however, there was a wide discrepancy in the political behaviour of the two linguistic groups. While 76 % of the members elected in English Montreal ridings between 1936 and 1956 were Liberals, the figure was only 47 % in French ridings. Since the population of the province was steadily becoming more concentrated in Montreal, the gap between the French and English in the city was reflected in the figures for the province as a whole.

After the election of 1936, which brought the Union Nationale to power, English Montrealers turned upon that party with a vengeance. Over the next five provincial elections not a single English riding in Montreal returned a Union Nationale member. This situation was particularly significant in as much as there were only two rural ridings, Brome and Pontiac, which still had predominantly English-speaking populations during this period. Accordingly, English Quebec came to be all but synonymous with English Montreal where there was no love lost between the English-speaking voter and the Union Nationale.

There can be little doubt that the turning point in the relations between the Union Nationale and English Montreal voters came with the start of World War II. It is interesting to note that the majority of English Montreal ridings supported the UN in the 1936 election, but that was before the start of the war and Duplessis' denunciation of Canada's war effort as an attack upon French Canada. In the election of 1939, which was fought on the strength of King's promise never to use conscription for overseas service, all Quebecers regardless of language supported the Liberals. The federal government ultimately went back on its promise by means of the 1942 plebiscite, providing Duplessis with the perfect opportunity to present himself as the sole defender of French-speaking interests. Such a platform had little appeal to English speakers who were more interested in winning the war, and the break between Duplessis and English Montrealers took place. This break did not heal in the post-war era; Duplessis consistently performed symbolic acts of defiance, such as the refusal of federal grants to Quebec's universities, so as to show himself the champion of French interests. English speakers were unimpressed, and for the first time since Confederation found themselves isolated from the French majority.

In their rejection of Duplessis, English speakers identified their interests with the provincial Liberal Party, and nothing that occurred between 1960 and 1976 changed this situation. After the election of 1970 there was not a single riding in the province outside of Montreal with an English-speaking majority, while in Montreal only one non-Liberal member was returned after 1970, William Shaw, who was elected under the Union Nationale banner in the 1976 election from the riding of Pointe-Claire. During the Duplessis era the UN was rejected by English-speaking voters because of its policies which often appeared hostile to their interests. The UN had changed by 1976, however, and the vote for Shaw was a rejection of both the Liberals and the Parti québécois for professing policies that were seen as too narrowly nationalistic. The antipathy towards the Liberals was due to its passage of legislation that restricted access to English schools, while the PQ's avowed goal of separation from the rest of Canada alienated nearly all English voters. The election of Shaw was exceptional, as few English speakers were prepared to abandon the Liberals and run the risk that a PQ member might be elected in their riding. By and large, in the post-1960 era English speakers identified their interests with the provincial Liberal Party. When the French population was also in the mood to vote Liberal then the two groups were in accord, but, as was the case in the election of 1976, when the majority of French speakers chose another option, the English were left with members, all of whom sat in the opposition. This was the price that the linguistic minority had to pay for having decided to vote as a bloc.

English speakers only began voting as a bloc following the start of World War II. Prior to 1939 there was little evidence of any striking differences in the way that French and English speakers voted. There is evidence, however, to indicate that as early as the election of 1919 a higher rate of abstention existed among English voters than among the French. The rate of abstention is the percentage of people on the voters' list who fail to vote. According to political scientist André Bernard, in provincial elections held between 1919 and 1970 "l'abstentionnisme moyen des anglophones... est habituellement deux fois plus élevé que celui des francophones." These differences existed in both urban and rural Quebec, and indicated a certain "défaut d'intégration de cette communauté minoritaire" into the political life of the province.[8] Interestingly, the only elections in which the rates of abstention among English speakers were similar to those for the French were those of 1939, 1966 and 1970. In each the English-speaking population perceived that its interests were threatened by certain militantly nationalistic politicians. In 1939 it was fear of the re-election of Duplessis in the midst of World War II, while in 1966 and 1970 the threat took the form of newly organized parties committed to Quebec's independence. Apparently, the perceived threat to their well-being in the post-1939 period pushed English speakers to vote as a bloc; it also encouraged them to stay away from the polls less frequently than had earlier been the case.

8. André Bernard, "L'Absentionnisme des électeurs de langue anglaise du Québec", in Daniel Latouche et al. eds , Le processus électoral au Québec (Montreal, 1976), pp. 160, 186.

b) *English Speakers and Federal Elections*

English Quebecers consistently registered relatively high rates of abstention in provincial elections to reflect their alienation from a political arena in which they made up the linguistic minority. By contrast, French-speaking Quebecers had the higher rates of abstention in federal elections as they found themselves in the minority. English speakers were more willing to vote in federal elections because on that level they formed part of the linguistic majority. Feeling less impotent, English Quebecers made the effort to vote in federal elections that they did not always make in provincial ones. [9]

The existence of a large English-speaking population outside Quebec not only encouraged English Quebecers to take the trouble to vote, but it also plays an important role in trying to understand the party preferences of English-speaking Quebecers in federal elections. In provincial politics, one can do little more than compare the preferences of English speakers with those of French-speaking Quebecers. However, in federal politics, there is the added possibility of comparing the behaviour of English Quebecers with that of their English-speaking counterparts elsewhere in Canada.

This added dimension of federal politics provides little help in understanding the behaviour of Quebecers in the federal elections held between 1867 and 1887. During these years the federal Liberal Party was struggling to get on its feet, and the Conservatives won clear majorities in all but one of the elections held. Within Quebec the Liberals were weak among both French and English speakers, as Table 10.2 indicates. There was relatively little difference in the level

---

9. *Ibid.*, pp. 155-159.

TABLE 10.2

Quebec and Federal Elections,
1867-1980

	% OF SEATS WON BY LIBERALS		
	1867-1887	1891-1935	1940-1980
Quebec	36	81	77
French	39	84	75
English	23	55	92
Montreal	21	73	94
French	25	93	94
English	17	51	92
Rest of Province	37	82	72
French	39	83	72
English	25	67	*

Source: *Canadian Parliamentary Guide* (Ottawa, 1984). The asterisk indicates that there were no ridings in the category.

of support for the Liberals among English and French-speaking Montrealers. Outside the city, the Liberals had greater success in French-speaking ridings than in English-speaking districts. This was most likely a reflection of the strongly pro-Conservative leanings of rural English speakers in the years after Confederation that was noted earlier in the discussion of provincial politics.

While the presence of an English-speaking majority outside the province apparently had little impact upon English speakers between 1867 and 1887, such was not the case in the federal elections held between 1891 and 1935. Twelve elections took place during these years, bringing both Liberals and Conservatives to power. While this period was not marked by the dominance of any one party, it was distinguished by the fact that in nine of the elections the party that won a plurality of the seats from Quebec was different from the party securing a plurality in the other provinces. Typical was the election of 1911 in which the Tories won a smashing victory outside Quebec but took only 27 of the 65 seats within the province. As for English-speaking Quebec, it tended to vote as did the rest of Canada. In the 1911 election four of the six predominantly English ridings in Quebec supported the Tories. The period between 1891 and 1935 was marked by a high level of support in Quebec for the federal Liberals, first under Laurier and then under King, but when the rest of the country kept its distance from these leaders English Quebecers followed suit. As a result, between 1891 and 1935 only 55 % of the MPs returned from English ridings in Quebec were Liberals, as opposed to 84 % for predominantly French ridings.

During this period the level of support for the Liberals was considerably higher among the English speakers outside Montreal than was the case in the city. However, even in rural areas the French ridings provided more support for the Liberals than was evident in the English ridings. Nevertheless, it is significant that while three English Montreal ridings joined the rest of Canada in 1917 in supporting the Union government and its policy of conscription, no other riding in Quebec did so, and that included the ridings of Brome and Pontiac which still had English majorities in that election. Because of the reorganization of the federal electoral map prior to the election of 1925, there were henceforth no predominantly English ridings in the province outside Montreal. English-speaking Quebec, for the purposes of federal elections, was reduced to the Island of Montreal where considerable French-English differences existed between 1891 and 1935.

The differences between English and French-speaking Montrealers all but disappeared, however, in the post-World War II era. Just as the start of the war and Duplessis' approach to it pushed the English Quebecers firmly into the Liberal camp in provincial politics, so did those events make English speakers into staunch Liberals on the federal level. For the four decades that followed, with very few exceptions, English Quebec was a Liberal stronghold no matter how the rest of Canada voted. This was a major break with the situation that had existed for a half century prior to the start of World War II, during which English Quebecers voted as did English speakers outside the province. Beginning with the war, however, there was a succession of provincial politicians who greatly worried English-speaking Quebecers. First there was Duplessis and then, in the 1960s and 1970, there was a series of *indépendantistes* who forced English Quebecers to narrow their horizons and vote for the party which seemed best able to respond to the nationalist challenge. English Quebec's saviours were to be found in the Liberal prime ministers, King, Saint-Laurent, Pearson and Trudeau, who consciously did battle with these forces of nationalism.

Between 1940 and 1980 English and French-speaking Quebecers voted similarly in federal elections but for very different reasons. For the French it was clear that their hopes for power on the federal level could only be satisfied within the Liberal party, given the frequently francophobic behaviour of the Tories. This support for the federal Liberals did not, of course, stand in the way of voting for the Union Nationale or the Parti québécois in provincial elections. The strategy of French-speaking Quebecers on both the federal and provincial levels was simply to return those who seemed most likely to advance their interests. For English speakers, by contrast, the strategy was to support those politicians most likely to ease their fears

Quebec Legislative Council
(Public Archives of Canada, PA-23976)

of the more assertive nationalistic elements that were emerging within French-speaking society. On both the federal and provincial levels this strategy made English speakers staunch Liberals. As will be seen in the next section, under most circumstances the unwritten rules that governed Quebec politics assured English speakers a certain representation in both the federal and provincial cabinets. By voting as a bloc, however, English speakers ran the risk of being left out in the cold if the Liberals were not in power.

2. English-Speaking Quebec and the Rules of the Game

Elections determine which party will form the government, but they do not necessarily determine the rules by which a political system operates. These rules can either be formally recorded in written documents, such as constitutions, or they can be the product of informal accords among the leaders of various groups within a society. In either case, however, such rules determine the range of options within which any government must operate. By concentrating on electoral results to the exclusion of an analysis of these rules and how they changed over time, one runs the risk of not fully understanding the role of any particular group within a political system. For English-speaking Quebec, for instance, the analysis of voting behaviour provided the means for viewing the frequent conflict between urban and rural interests. In the post-World War II era these rural interests had all but ceased to exist, while English-speaking Montrealers addressed themselves to the challenge posed by the Union Nationale and the Parti québécois. Nevertheless, there are further insights into the place of English speakers within the political system on both the federal and provincial levels that can only be gained by examining the rules of the game and how they evolved after 1867.

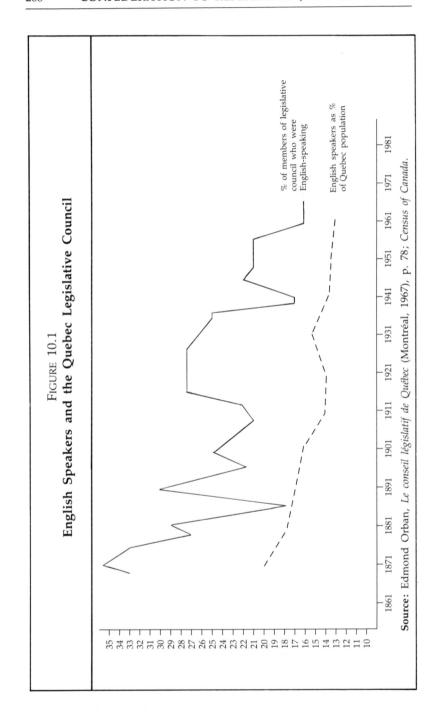

FIGURE 10.1

English Speakers and the Quebec Legislative Council

% of members of legislative council who were English-speaking

English speakers as % of Quebec population

Source: Edmond Orban, *Le conseil législatif de Québec* (Montréal, 1967), p. 78; *Census of Canada.*

The formal place accorded to English-speaking Quebec within the new Canadian political system was laid down in the BNA Act. In terms of federal institutions, there were few explicit guarantees regarding English speakers, since the politicians assumed that the English majority outside Quebec could ultimately defend the interests of Quebec's minority. The one exception to this rule occurred in the case of Quebec's representatives in the Senate, each of whom was to be appointed to represent a specific part of the province. The purpose of this arrangement was to assure representation for such English enclaves as the Eastern Townships. Significantly, no other province was subject to such a condition regarding its appointees to the Senate.

More numerous were the clauses inserted into the BNA Act to protect the English minority at the provincial level. In 1867 Quebec was the only province to have an upper house, the legislative council, whose members were to be appointed by the provincial government on the same geographical basis as the appointments to the Senate. The legislative council was designed to protect the English minority from possible abuses by the elected assembly.[10] Further protection was provided by Article 80 which froze the boundaries of twelve ridings for elections to the assembly.[11] These ridings in the Eastern Townships and the Ottawa Valley had all had English majorities in the 1850s, and their boundaries could only be altered with the approval of a majority of the members who represented the ridings.

10. Edouard Orban, *Le conseil législatif du Québec* (Montreal, 1967), pp. 40-42.
11. Jean-Charles Bonenfant, "Les douze circonscriptions électorales 'privilégiées' du Québec", *Cahiers de géographie du Québec* (1962), pp. 161-166.

All of these formal provisions concerned the political influence of English speakers residing outside Montreal. Such a preoccupation is hardly surprising, given the fact that the English-speaking population in both the Eastern Townships and the Quebec City region declined considerably during the 1860s. Nevertheless, precisely because of the loss of demographic strength by such English-speaking groups outside Montreal, these various provisions of the BNA Act lost their meaning over time. The clause regarding appointments to the Senate remains part of the constitution, but it no longer serves its intended purpose because of the francization of all regions outside Montreal. In 1867, 38 % of Quebec's Senate seats belonged to English speakers, a figure that steadily declined to 25 % by 1930 and 17 % by 1960. This decline roughly paralleled the decline within the Quebec population of the percentage which had English as its mother tongue.

In terms of the special status accorded to English Quebec within provincial institutions, once again the power of declining numbers took its toll over time. As Figure 10.1 indicates, the legislative council generally succeeded in its goal of over-representing English Quebecers. Nevertheless, the place of the minority both within the population as a whole and within the council had declined to such a point by the 1960s that no complaint of any importance was registered by the English population when the council was abolished by the Quebec legislature in 1968. Nor was there much of a reaction to the suppression of Article 80 in 1970. The clause had already lost some of its original intent by the time of Confederation, as three of the twelve protected ridings had French majorities. The English representatives still had enough power in 1890 to approve the division of the predominantly French riding of Richmond-Wolfe into two ridings, one English and one French. At the same time they blocked the division of the heavily French riding of Ottawa into three French-speaking ridings. By 1901, however, the majority of the protected ridings were French, and the original intent of the clause could no longer be carried out, with the result that few mourned its passing.

No political party, regardless of its programme, was entirely free to change these rules until transformations in the English population allowed a new consensus to emerge that facilitated the abolition of both the legislative council and Article 80. Similarly, changes in the English population led to changes in the informal understandings that existed regarding the place of English Quebecers in both the federal and provincial cabinets.

On the federal level, the process of cabinet formation was a complicated one in which a multitude of interests had to be recognized. Normally, it began by dividing the total number of available positions among the various provinces. In forming Canada's first cabinet in 1867, Macdonald wanted no more than thirteen members, four of whom would come from Quebec. The decision then had to be made as to how many of the four Quebec posts would go to English speakers. English Quebec could hardly be totally ignored, and yet to give half of Quebec's cabinet posts to English speakers was unthinkable. Accordingly, English Quebec was to have one seat in the original cabinet, even though it had two strong candidates, D'Arcy McGee and Alexander Galt. The former was the representative of the English-Catholic population, while the latter was a Townshipper with strong ties with the Montreal business community. Recognizing the superior power of the interests represented by Galt, McGee stepped aside so as to leave the way clear for Galt's appointment as Canada's first finance minister.

By Laurier's time the cabinet had expanded to the point that seven positions could be allotted to Quebec. In forming his first cabinet in 1896, Laurier gave three of these posts to English speakers. As a percentage of the Quebec seats in the cabinet, this was the largest representation that English speakers would ever have. This reflected Laurier's belief that, as a French-speaking prime minister, he could stand up for French interests to allow greater representation for the English. Once he decided to give three positions to English speakers, Laurier then used them to satisfy various elements within that diverse population. Richard Dobell was appointed to represent business interests, while Charles Fitzpatrick represented the Irish and Sydney Fisher, the Eastern Townships. The appointment of Fisher, in particular, proved to be important, for his tenure marked the end of the Townships' claim upon a seat in the cabinet. [12] From the time of Galt the region had been assured a seat in the cabinet, but now the rules of the game could be changed to reflect the shrinking English-speaking population of the Eastern Townships.

By the time of the formation of Mackenzie King's first cabinet in 1921, the declining influence of the English-speaking population was even more evident. King had originally wanted to appoint five cabinet ministers from Quebec, one of whom would be an English speaker. There was some pressure on King to increase the total number of Quebec posts to six in order to give a second seat to an English Quebecer. In the end, however, French-speaking interests from the province prevailed. There were six Quebec cabinet ministers, but only one was an English speaker.

---

12. Neatby, p. 123.

In forming his 1935 cabinet there was no question in King's mind of English Quebecers holding more than one seat, but the dilemma that he faced was to find a suitable person to fill the role. Historian Frederick Gibson has noted that there was no "obvious choice for the role of cabinet representative of the English-speaking population of Quebec."[13] Of the names first suggested there was no representative of the Montreal business community, a clear indication of the loss of the power that it had earlier held. In the end the English Quebec appointment went to Charles G. (Chubby) Power, but, as Gibson has pointed out, Power was in the cabinet to "represent the Irish population of Canada rather than the English-speaking population of Quebec. The 600,000 English of Montreal and the Eastern Townships received no other representation."[14]

Gibson's grasp of figures is troublesome, since there were fewer than 450,000 English speakers in all of Quebec in the 1930s. Nevertheless, he was correct in recognizing the discernible decline of English Quebec's influence by the 1930s. With its shrinking English population, an area such as the Eastern Townships had lost its seat in the cabinet early in the century, and now it had even become possible to ignore the once powerful English Montreal business community. At the same time that the Toronto Stock Exchange was surpassing that of Montreal in terms of the value of shares traded, Montreal's business leaders were being locked out of the cabinet. Nothing that occurred between 1935 and 1980 revitalized the place of English speakers in the federal cabinet. In the Trudeau cabinet formed after the election of 1980, there were eight

---

13. Frederick Gibson, ed., *Cabinet Formation and Bicultural Relations* (Ottawa, 1970), p. 110.
14. *Ibid.*, p. 140.

Chubby Power
(Norman Ward, ed.,
A Party Politician)

Christopher Dunkin
(Public Archives of Canada,
PA-26325)

ministers from Quebec, but only Donald Johnston was an English speaker. The informal rules by which the federal cabinet positions were apportioned had changed considerably between 1867 and 1980 to reflect changes in the English-speaking population. In 1867 Alexander Galt was a powerful figure in the cabinet representing both the Eastern Townships and Montreal business interests. Neither of these concerns could warrant representation by 1980 so that a relatively powerless cabinet minister sufficed for the English-speaking population.

The declining influence of English-speaking Quebec was also evident in the process of forming Quebec cabinets between 1867 and 1980. In terms of their percentage of the seats in the cabinet, English speakers have seen a steady decline from the situation in the 1890s when they occupied nearly half of all posts. Provincial cabinets were small during this time, and it was customary that there be three English-speaking ministers, two Protestant and one Catholic. Accordingly, it was not difficult for English speakers to hold a larger percentage of cabinet positions than their numbers warranted. However, by 1920, in the face of a declining English-speaking population outside Montreal, one of the Protestant seats was taken away. By 1944, given the limited support of the English for the Union Nationale, Duplessis selected only one English-speaking minister. With the election of the Parti québécois in 1976, this gradual decline was completed as English speakers found themselves for the first time excluded from the cabinet, a situation that was made inevitable by their total support for the provincial Liberals.

The decline of English influence within the Quebec cabinet was evident, however, not only in terms of the number of seats held but also in terms of the positions that were held. For instance, the power of the English business elite was such that the position of Provincial Treasurer (equivalent to the Minister of Finance) was essentially reserved for English speakers between 1867 and 1944. When Joseph-Edouard Cauchon was asked to form the first Quebec government in 1867, he made the mistake of ignoring the power of English business interests by proposing a French speaker to serve as Provincial Treasurer. Under severe pressure from all directions, Cauchon ultimately withdrew his original nomination and offered the post of Treasurer to Christopher Dunkin who refused the offer because of Cauchon's opposition to the expansion of Protestant educational rights. Unable to fill the Treasurer's position, Cauchon abandoned the task of forming a government to P.J.O. Chauveau who became Quebec's first premier. Not having alienated the English-speaking population as had Cauchon, Chauveau was able to secure Dunkin as his Treasurer, thus beginning a long tradition,[15] a tradition that was still going strong in 1930 when the premier of the time, Louis-Alexandre Taschereau, explained his choice of Gordon Scott as Treasurer on the following grounds: "We wished to continue the Quebec tradition by confiding the Treasury to one of our compatriotes of the English language."[16]

There were exceptions to the English control of the Treasurer's office prior to 1944, but after that date not a single English speaker held that position. Other cabinet posts were subsequently identified as belonging to the English. Such was the case for the position of Minister of Mines under Duplessis and that of Minister of Revenue in the various governments of the

---

15. Marcel Hamelin, *Les premières années du parlementarisme québécois* (Quebec, 1974), pp. 10-14.
16. Jean Hamelin et Louise Beaudouin, "Les cabinets provinciaux, 1867-1967", in Richard Desrosiers, ed., *Le personnel politique québécois* (Montreal, 1972), p. 99.

1960s. However, neither of these posts came close to providing the sort of power inherent in the finance portfolio. The withdrawal of this post from English control was a further change in the unwritten rules of the political system that could be made because of the declining influence of the English-speaking population.

3. Conclusion

Many of the changes in the position of English Quebec within the political system were gradual ones which mirrored changes in the place of the minority within the population of Quebec. This was true of most aspects of the decline of English Quebecers within both the federal and provincial cabinets. Similarly, in the face of a relatively declining place within the Quebec population and an absolute decline outside Montreal, English Quebec representation in both the House of Commons and the National Assembly was greatly altered in the post-Confederation period. As Table 10.3 indicates, on both levels of government by the end of the 1970s English Quebecers constituted a much smaller percentage of the province's parliamentarians than they had in 1867; at the same time the English representation that remained was solely from the Island of Montreal.

TABLE 10.3

English Quebec and Parliamentary Institutions,
1867-1980

	# ENG. REPRE-SENTA-TIVES	% TOTAL QUEBEC REPRE-SENTA-TIVES	ENGLISH REPRESENTATIVES FROM EACH REGION				
			Eastern Town-ships	Ottawa Valley	Mon-treal	Que. City	Gaspé
National Assembly							
1867	16	25	8	3	3	1	1
1976	7	6	—	—	7	—	—
House of Commons							
1867	17	26	10	4	2	1	—
1980	7	9	—	—	7	—	—

Source: Québec, Bibliothèque de la Législature, *Répertoire des parlemen-taires québécois* (Quebec, 1980); *Canadian Parliamentary Guide* (Ottawa, 1984).

These changes were gradual, but there were other aspects of English Quebec's status in the political system that changed abruptly in the post-World War II period. For instance, in terms of their behaviour at the polls in both federal and provincial elections after 1939, English Quebecers consistently voted as a bloc, something they had only rarely done previously. After 1939 English Quebec placed nearly all of its votes at the disposal of the federal and provincial Liberal parties, a situation that was dangerous for a minority in a deteriorating state. In the post-war era, English Quebecers were to find themselves excluded from representation in the governments of Canada and Quebec when the Liberals were out of power; and even when the Liberals were in power the minority's leverage was limited, as Liberal leaders, federal and provincial alike, could take the support of the English-speaking population for granted. Robert Bourassa calculated that English Quebecers would not abandon him despite the introduction of language legislation in 1974. That he was largely correct is evident from the fact that only a single English riding abandoned the Liberals in the election of 1976.

English Quebec was ill-prepared to cope with this loss of power within both the federal and provincial governments. The English-speaking population had never systematically organized itself to lobby outside the parliamentary institutions in support of its interests. Whenever such lobbying was required it had been done by the members of Montreal's business elite. These men, who were usually Protestant and of either English or Scottish origin, had considerable difficulty in speaking for a population divided by ethnic, religious, class and regional differences. Nevertheless, at times such as the period leading up to Confederation, the business elite had been able to use its muscle to secure political concessions of some use to most English speakers. However, in the post World War II era, when English Quebec's power within parliamentary institutions was on the decline, so too was the strength of the business elite, a fact attested to by the loss of the provincial finance portfolio in 1944. Accordingly, by the mid-1940s English Quebec found itself with limited means to influence political events. This impotence, which was particularly evident in the language legislation passed in the 1970s, was a reflection of the various changes that the English-speaking population had undergone since Confederation.

SELECT BIBLIOGRAPHY

Bernard, André. "L'abstentionnisme des électeurs de langue anglaise du Québec", in Daniel Latouche et al. eds., *Le processus électoral au Québec*. Montreal, 1976.

Bonenfant, Jean-Charles. "Les douze circonscriptions privilégiées du Québec", *Cahiers de géographie du Québec*, (1962), 161-66.

Desrosiers, Richard, ed. *Le personnel politique québécois*. Montreal, 1972.

Gibson, Frederick, ed. *Cabinet Formation and Bicultural Relations*. Ottawa, 1970.

Hamelin, Jean, Jacques Letarte et Marcel Hamelin. "Les élections provinciales dans le Québec", *Cahiers de géographie du Québec* (1959-60).

Postscript
English Quebec
at the Start of a New Era

The goal of this book has been to identify certain patterns in the history of English-speaking Quebec. Some of the characteristics of this population, such as the conflict between English speakers of different social classes, have been evident since the time of the Conquest. Other characteristics germane to the post-Confederation period differed from those that had predominated prior to 1867. For instance, before Confederation English speakers made up an ever-growing percentage of the Quebec population, while after 1867 this percentage steadily declined. Similarly, the pre-Confederation period saw large concentrations of English speakers in various parts of the province, while the post-1867 era witnessed the progressive concentration of this population in the Montreal area. Since certain significant characteristics of the English-speaking population prior to 1867 were transformed in the post-Confederation era, this study has been divided into two parts with Confederation serving as the dividing line between two eras.

By the start of the 1980s, however, English-speaking Quebec found itself at the start of what appeared to be a new era. A third period in its history

seemed about to begin because of certain unprecedented changes whose roots could hardly be traced back
further than the 1960s. Older trends, such as the
decline of the British element within the English-
speaking population and the concentration of this
population in the Montreal area, seemed likely to
continue. At the same time, however, there were other, newer trends emerging, such as the unprecedented
growth of bilingualism.

Information regarding the rate of bilingualism
among English mother tongue Quebecers only became
available with the appearance of the 1971 census.
There are, however, reliable figures regarding bilingualism among Quebecers of British origin from 1921
on. What is striking is the lack of change in the
percentage of those that were bilingual as recorded in
the five censuses from 1921 to 1961. In each, the
percentage of British origin Quebecers who were bilingual was, with only one exception, 29 %, and in that
one case the figure was 30 %. Throughout most of the
twentieth century the rate of bilingualism was invari-
able, but this trend began to dissolve in the face of the
changes that transformed Quebec society as a whole in
the 1960s. The percentage of British origin Quebecers
who were bilingual jumped to 34 % in 1971 and, even
more dramatically, to 47 % by 1981. For the English
mother tongue population as a whole, this figure was
37 % in 1971 and 53 % by 1981. This was probably the
first time in the history of English-speaking Quebec
that a majority of that population could claim an ability
to converse in French.

There were two factors responsible for the growth
of bilingualism among English-speaking Quebecers,
one forming part of the older trends described elsewhere in this study and the other, a complete departure from the past. The older trend was the continued
departure of unilingual English speakers, which result-

ed in an increase in the level of bilingualism among those who remained. The departure of English speakers from the province had been a regular part of the history of this population since the mid-1800s. However, in the 1970s the level of these departures to other provinces picked up, playing a role in the decline of the number of English speakers by 11 % during the decade. Among Quebecers of British origin there was an absolute decline of 17 % during the same period. As Table 11.1 indicates, the British losses were particularly large among those who were unilingual. In part this was the simple departure of those least capable of coping with the new circumstances in Quebec. In addition, however, the decline in the number of unilingual British origin Quebecers was the result of the efforts of a significant number of these people to make themselves bilingual. This aspect of the growth of bilingualism was unprecedented in the history of English-speaking Quebec and was evident both in the workplace and in the schools.

TABLE 11.1

Changes in the British Origin Population of Quebec, 1971-1981

	1971	1981	CHANGE
British Origin	640,040	528,842	−111,198 (−17 %)
Bilingual	215,535	248,283	+ 32,784 (+15 %)
Unilingual	424,505	280,559	−143,946 (−34 %)

Source: *Census of Canada.*

In the 1970s English speakers determined to stay in the province made serious efforts to provide both themselves and their chidren with the means to function in French. The absolute increase in the number of

Founding meeting of Montreal Center Chapter of Alliance
Quebec, 25 February 1982
(Alliance Quebec)

Headquarters of the Protestant School Board of Greater Montreal
(Archives de la Ville de Montréal)

bilingual Quebecers of British origin was, in part, a reflection of the realization by English speakers of the need to work in French if they hoped to succeed on the Quebec job market. In assessing changes in the male Montreal labour force between 1971 and 1978, Jac-André Boulet has found that the growth of bilingualism among English speakers was "not solely the result of a relative exodus of unilingual Anglophones from the job market." Rather, "the group's new language configuration" was also the product of the newfound ability to operate in French by heretofore unilingual English speakers.[1]

Those English speakers who chose to stay also played a role in the rise of bilingualism in their ranks through the choices they made regarding their children's education. Within the Protestant School Board of Greater Montreal (PSBGM), the board with the largest number of English mother tongue students in the province, the situation at the start of the 1970s was much as it had been for decades. Out of over 60,000 students only 5 % were in French schools or French immersion programmes within the English schools. By the start of the 1984-1985 school year, however, nearly 40 % of the board's students came into one of these two categories. According to the PSBGM's own estimate, two-thirds of the students in its French schools were ineligible to attend English schools according to the provisions of Bill 101.[2] Most were the children of Haitians or other non-English-speaking Quebecers. When these numbers were subtracted from the student population in the PSBGM's schools, the percentage of English-speaking students in French schools or French immersion programmes fell to 30 %, but this was still a dramatic change from the situation that had existed at the start of the 1970s.

1. Boulet, *Language and Earnings*, p. 6.
2. PSBGM, *Annual Report for 1980-1*.

TABLE 11.2

French Language Programmes in the PSBGM,
1970-1984

		FRENCH IMMERSION		FRENCH SCHOOLS	
Year	Total Student Population	Number	% of Total	Number	% of Total
1970-1	60,476	1779	2.9	1361	2.3
1984-5	31,145	5753	18.5	6658	21.4

Source: PSBGM, Student Enrollments as of 30 September of each school year.

It seems unlikely that these trends in education will be reversed in the foreseeable future. The trend away from the traditional English language school seems likely to continue, with parents who have conscientiously chosen to stay in Quebec providing their children with the means to do the same. As unilingual Quebecers either die or move away, these graduates of the various French programmes will most likely contribute to a steady increase in the rate of bilingualism among English speakers. Moreover, these students will take with them a different attitude towards life in Quebec than was maintained by earlier generations of English speakers. In their study of the attitudes of students in French immersion programmes, Wallace Lambert and Richard Tucker have found some significant contrasts with the views of students in the traditional English programme. The immersion students "showed a more positive attitude towards French-speaking Canadians and a greater willingness to make contacts with French-speaking friends." The immersion students also expressed a greater desire to remain in Quebec. [3]

---

3. Wallace Lambert and Richard Tucker, "Graduates of Early French Immersion", in Caldwell and Waddell, *The English of Quebec*, p. 274.

The determination of English speakers to adjust to the changed circumstances of life in Quebec by the start of the 1980s was evident in the growth of bilingualism in their ranks. Similarly, this adjustment to a new environment was visible in the emergence of a new form of political organization. The previous chapter described the process whereby, at the start of the 1980s, English Quebec had become politically impotent because of its total identification with both the Quebec and the federal Liberal parties and its failure to develop any means of lobbying outside the parliamentary institutions in support of its interests. In this context the establishment of Alliance Quebec in 1982 as the lobbying agent for English speakers was an important event. Following the decline of the English-speaking population in the 1970s, the election of Parti québécois governments in 1976 and 1981, and the holding of the referendum on sovereignty-association in 1980, diverse elements within the English-speaking population were prepared for the first time in their history to sit down to identify their common interests. To even make this effort meant that English speakers had come to grips with their political impotence and were committed to remaining in the province and bettering their lot.

The establishment of Alliance Quebec, like the growth of bilingualism, was symbolic of certain new trends in the behaviour of English-speaking Quebecers which did not have deep roots in the history of this population. One is tempted to see these trends in a positive light as English speakers tried to cope with the changes that transformed Quebec society after 1960. It seems reasonable to envision an English-speaking population which, in the years to come, will be increasingly bilingual and more adept at political organization.

At the same time, however, this population will have to cope with the continuation of the trends that have been described throughout this study. The most significant of these pertains to the ease with which English speakers can leave Quebec to seek better economic prospects elsewhere in North America. By the start of the 1980s it had long been clear that economic power in Canada was firmly concentrated in Toronto. In the process Montreal was reduced to the status of a regional centre whose offices largely catered to a Quebec market. Such offices tend to function in French, which means that there will be little incentive in the future for English speakers to come to Quebec. English speakers already residing in the province will be in a position to compete for French positions owing to their increased bilingualism. It seems inevitable, however, that a certain number of English speakers, even though bilingual, will judge that their prospects might be better elsewhere and will leave the province.

Given the increased power of French within the Quebec economy, there will be few English speakers coming to Quebec to take the places of those departing, and there will be little incentive for Quebecers who have neither French nor English as their mother tongue to pass English along to their children. In addition to the increased bilingualism of English speakers one is likely to see more frequent marriages between English and French speakers. The children of these marriages will be increasingly likely to have French as their mother tongue, thus further reducing the ranks of English speakers in future generations.

A significant number of English speakers were still residing in Quebec at the start of the 1980s, approximately 700,000, but this figure seems likely to decline in years to come. Even though its numbers will continue to decline, English-speaking Quebec will benefit from its easy access to television and radio services in its own language. By sharing the language of the majority of North Americans, English speakers will never have to feel the isolation that contributed to the assimilation of many French speakers in the other provinces of Canada. In a different manner, however, the North American context works to the disadvantage of the continued survival of English-speaking Quebec. English speakers have never had difficulty in moving to other parts of the continent, and they are likely to continue to leave the province in years to come, particularly as their numbers become too small to support the full range of institutions to which they have become accustomed. As Robert Sellar observed at the turn of the century, once the institutions of a population begin to deteriorate there is little that can be done to keep it in place. This is particularly true for a population which, since the beginning of its history, has been extremely mobile.

Appendix
Suggestions for Further Reading and Research

Since this book was partly conceived as a tool for stimulating further interest in the history of English-speaking Quebec, this appendix has been included to provide some direction for both the casual reader and the serious researcher.

1. Suggestions for Further Reading

There is no dearth of secondary literature pertaining to the history of English-speaking Quebec. Indeed, a yet-to-be-published bibliography on the subject lists over 2,500 items.[1] Much of this material is of only limited value as it deals with very specific issues in a totally descriptive rather than analytical way. Nevertheless, there are some published studies, a certain number of which are listed below, that are well worth reading by anyone who wants to delve more deeply into the subject.

---

1. Brendan O'Donnell, *A History of English-Speaking Quebec: An Annotated Bibliography*.

For the period immediately following the Conquest, the best source is probably A.L. Burt's *The Old Province of Quebec* (Minneapolis, 1933). Although written over half a century ago, Burt's book is still worth consulting for its attention to the political conflicts within the English-speaking elite during the last third of the eighteenth century. Also of value for an understanding of the economic and political ambitions of some of the earliest English-speaking leaders is Donald Creighton's *The Empire of the St. Lawrence* (Toronto, 1956). Originally published only four years after Burt's work, Creighton's study has been disdained by many for its blatant anti-French tone. Nevertheless, it has much to offer regarding the machinations of certain English-speaking businessmen between 1760 and 1850.

There are also a number of interesting studies of English speakers in the pre-Confederation period who wielded much less power than the men discussed by Burt and Creighton. The arrival of British immigrants prior to 1867 is chronicled by Helen Cowan in her *British Emigration to North America* (Toronto, 1961). The Irish made up the largest group within this immigrant population, and their situation near the bottom of Quebec's economic ladder is discussed by H.C. Pentland in his *Labour and Capital in Canada* (Toronto, 1981). Another group of non-elite English speakers, the fishermen of the Gaspé, is given attention in *Histoire de la Gaspésie* by Jules Bélanger, Marc Desjardins and Yves Frenette (Montreal, 1981). English speakers involved in the pre-Confederation lumber trade are discussed by Arthur Lower in his *Great Britain's Woodyard* (Montreal, 1973), while J.I. Little has described the lives of farmers in the Eastern Townships in his excellent article, "The Social and Economic Development of Settlers in Two Quebec Townships, 1851-70" (*Canadian Papers in Rural History*, I, 89-113).

As for the political behaviour of English speakers, there are few useful sources for either the pre- or the post-Confederation periods. Regarding the period prior to 1867, two of the more informative books pertain to Confederation. In his *The French Canadian Idea of Confederation* (Toronto, 1981) Arthur Silver provides a good discussion of the provisions secured in the BNA Act by the English-speaking minority. The speeches of English Quebec's political leaders in the debate over the Quebec Resolutions can be found in P.B. Waite, ed., *The Confederation Debates in the Province of Canada* (Toronto, 1963). These speeches make interesting reading as they reflect the diversity of the pre-Confederation English-speaking population. As for the period after 1867, one of the more interesting studies is André Bernard's, "L'abstentionnisme des électeurs de langue anglaise du Québec" (Daniel Latouche, et al., eds., *Le processus électoral au Québec* (Montréal, 1976), pp. 155-66).

On non-political issues, however, there is a wealth of material pertaining to the post-Confederation period. For instance, the changing ethnic composition of the English-speaking population is touched upon in various works. Regarding English speakers of British origin, the most useful study is Lloyd Reynolds' *The British Immigrant* (Toronto, 1935). The integration of immigrants not of British origin into the English-speaking population is discussed in various demographic studies such as Gary Caldwell's *A Demographic Profile of the English-speaking Population of Quebec, 1921-71* (Quebec, 1974) and *The Demolinguistic Situation in Canada* by Réjean Lachapelle and Jacques Henripin (Montreal, 1982).

The post-Confederation decline of the English-speaking population outside Montreal has also received considerable attention, most notably the decline experienced in the Eastern Townships. The most interesting work in this regard is Robert Sellar's *The Tragedy of Quebec* (Toronto, 1974). Originally published in 1907, this book contains the reactions of a Hunting-

don newspaperman who saw the region transformed
from a predominantly English one to a predominantly
French one. The 1974 reprint also contains an excellent
introduction by historian Robert Hill which serves to
place Sellar's remarks in the context of the times.
Similarly useful are two articles in the *Journal of Canadian Studies*: J.I. Little's "Watching the Frontier Disappear: English-Speaking Reaction to French Canadian
Colonization in the Eastern Townships, 1844-1890"
(XV, 93-111) and the present author's "The Transformation of the Eastern Townships of Richard William
Heneker, 1855-1902" (XIX, 32-49). For an analysis of
English-speaking Quebec's current status outside
Montreal, see Gary Caldwell's *Le Québec anglophone hors
de la région de Montréal dans les années soixante-dix* (Quebec, 1980).

The post-Confederation economic power of the
leading English-speaking businessmen has been described in numerous works, Tom Naylor's *The History of
Canadian Business, 1867-1914* (Toronto, 1975) for example. As for the lot of those English speakers with far
less power, see Terry Copp's *The Anatomy of Poverty:
The Condition of the Working Class in Montreal, 1897-1929*
(Toronto, 1974). There are also several works that have
tried to situate English speakers within the social structure of Quebec in the post-World War II period. In
their article "Inter-Generational Mobility in the Province of Quebec" (*Canadian Journal of Economic and Political Science*, XXIII, 57-68), Yves de Jocas and Guy Rocher
have presented a highly interesting comparison of the
rates of inter-generational mobility experienced by English and French-speaking Quebecers in the immediate
post-war era. This study was replicated for a subsequent generation by Jacques Dofny and Muriel Garon-
Audy in their article, "Mobilités professionnelles au
Québec" (*Sociologie et Société*, I, 277-301). The relative
wages earned by English and French speakers are
assessed by Jac-André Boulet in his *Language and Earn-*

ings in Montreal (Ottawa, 1980) and by Robert Lacroix and François Vaillancourt in their *Les revenus et la langue au Québec* (Quebec, 1980).

To this point, all of the works that have been cited are published studies. There are also, however, a number of interesting unpublished theses that warrant attention and which can readily be obtained through inter-library loan. For instance, the issue of the political behaviour of English speakers, which received so little attention in the published material, has been treated in an interesting manner in four dissertations: F. Murray Greenwood, "The Development of a Garrison Mentality Among the English of Lower Canada, 1793-1811" (Ph.D., University of British Columbia, 1970); Philip Goldring, "British Colonists and Imperial Interests in Lower Canada, 1830-41" (D. Phil., University of London, 1978); Pierre Corbeil, "Les députés anglophones et le premier gouvernement du Québec de 1867 à 1871" (Ph.D., Université de Montréal, 1978); Brendan O'Donnell, "Consociationalism, English Quebec and the Chauveau Ministry, 1867-1872: A Study of Political Accommodation" (M.A., Wilfrid Laurier University, 1980). The issue of English-speaking education is another one that has received relatively little attention in the published literature. Of this published material, the most useful is probably Nathan Mair's *The Quest for Quality in the Protestant Public Schools of Quebec* (Quebec, 1980). Equally valuable are two theses written by Keith Hunte: "The Development of a System of Education in Canada East, 1841-67" (M.A. McGill University, 1962) and "The Ministry of Public Instruction in Quebec, 1867-1875" (Ph.D., McGill University, 1965). Of a number of theses pertaining to the Irish in Quebec, the most interesting is D.S. Cross' "The Irish in Montreal, 1867-96" (M.A., McGill University, 1969). Finally, the decline of the English-speaking population in the Gaspé is interestingly discussed by Roger Clarke in his "In Them Days: The Breakdown of a Traditional Fishing Economy in an English Village on the Gaspé Coast" (Ph.D., McGill University, 1973).

2. Suggestions for further research

In the face of a meager body of high quality literature, there are nearly unlimited possibilities for interesting research projects on the history of English-speaking Quebec. In the sections that follow I have noted five different possible areas for future research that appear well worth pursuing in the light of the issues discussed in the text.

a) *Demographic Issues*

The major primary source used in this study was the Canadian census, particularly the published reports that have been issued on a decennial basis since 1851. These reports provide a wealth of information regarding such issues as the age structure of the population, its spatial distribution, its fertility and mortality rates, as well as its distribution among various ethnic, religious and linguistic groupings. So plentiful is the information available in these volumes that this study used only a small part of it. There are still questions of considerable importance that remain to be asked: were French families larger than English ones? Precisely where did English speakers go when they left regions such as the Eastern Townships? How has the age structure of the English-speaking population evolved over time? These and many other questions could be considered by using the published census reports.

Such reports were compiled from the information collected on each individual by the census takers. The forms filled in by these enumerators are available to researchers for each census held prior to 1891. (The 1891 census becomes available in 1991 according to the federal government's policy of restricting access to such records for one hundred years.) While the published reports indicate how many people of Irish origin lived in Quebec in 1871 and how many Catholics resided in the province, they do not explain how many Quebecers were both Irish and Catholic. However, by using the enumerators' forms it would be possible, although very time consuming, to figure this out by looking at the information pertaining to each individual. Developing such basic demographic data is essential to increasing our understanding of the history of English-speaking Quebec.

b) *The Voting Behaviour of English Speakers*

The analysis of voting behaviour presented in chapters five and ten could be greatly improved upon by examining the number of votes recorded for each candidate in each poll in each election and by considering this information in the light of demographic data available from the census. It might then be possible to see whether there was a relationship (controlling for the impact of other factors) between the linguistic makeup of an area and its voting behaviour. It is only through such research that we can hope to understand whether English speakers tended to vote differently from their French-speaking counterparts.

c) *History of English Education in Quebec*

It was argued throughout this study that the evolution of English-language education in Quebec mirrored changes in the English-speaking population. Much more research needs to be done, however, to understand all the various aspects of the history of English education in the province. The annual reports of the Superintendent of Public Instruction from the mid-1800s up to the establishment of the Ministry of Education in the 1960s provide a wealth of information regarding the backgrounds of the students who attended English schools. These same reports also generally contain the deliberations of the Protestant and Catholic committees of the Council of Public Instruction. By examining these records one can see the ongoing debates regarding the structure of education in Quebec. For the particularly ambitious researcher, there is also the massive and nearly untouched collection of education-related documents housed at the Archives Nationales du Québec in Quebec City.

d) *Local History*

The experiences of English speakers varied considerably from region to region, and frequently there were significant variations in the histories of predominantly English communities within a given region. Accordingly, there is a great need for a careful analysis of the evolution of those communities where English-speaking populations were important at a given time. This process can begin by building on the numerous local histories that have already been written on areas that were home to large numbers of English speakers. Too frequently these histories do little more than make reference to the initial settlement of the community and the contribution of its leading citizens. Future historians need to go further and consider such issues as the ethnic composition of the local English-speaking population and the economic opportunities that existed. Then, by comparing different types of communities it will be possible to answer such questions as why some English-speaking communities outside Montreal survived longer than others.

e) Social History

This study has considered English speakers who were distinguished from one another by factors such as religion, ethnicity and class. All of these factors warrant further research. For instance, the role of religion as a force in the history of English-speaking Quebec is barely understood even though there is general recognition of the role of religion within French-speaking Quebec. In terms of ethnicity, there is still much work to be done to distinguish the experiences of the different British origin groups as well as to look more carefully at the process by which people without English as their mother tongue were attracted by that language. As for the class distinctions within the English-speaking population, much remains to be done to understand the lives of English speakers who laboured in the factories of the province. To what extent were particular positions in industry earmarked for members of specific ethnic or linguistic groups? One thinks here of the way in which certain jobs in heavy industry at the start of the twentieth century seemed to be reserved for Quebecers of British origin. Was the experience of the English-speaking members of the working class demonstrably different from that of their French-speaking counterparts?

A further question that needs to be addressed by researchers pertains to the history of English-speaking women in Quebec. Given the general absence of literature on the subject, little mention was made in the text regarding the lives of English-speaking women. Nevertheless, there are some reasons to believe that research into the experiences of English-speaking women will reveal a history far different from that experienced by their French-speaking counterparts. Most English-speaking women were not subject to the edicts of the Catholic church. As a result they tended to have access to better educational facilities and played a key role in the drive to secure the vote for women in Quebec. In addition, because of the central role of English in the major offices located in Montreal, English-speaking women in the pre-World War II era had a better chance for clerical employment than did French speakers whose lack of fluency in English left them concentrated in poor paying factory jobs. Issues such as these could profitably be pursued in future studies.

Index

— Q —

— R —

— S —

LES PUBLICATIONS DE L'I.Q.R.C.

2. Gary Caldwell et Éric Waddell, dir. *Les anglophones du Québec: de majoritaires à minoritaires.* Coll. « Identité et changements culturels » n° 1, 1982, 482 pages.. 14,00 $

3. Gary Caldwell et Éric Waddell, editors. *The English of Quebec: from majority to minority status.* Coll. « Identité et changements culturels » n° 2, 1982, 466 pages .... 14,00 $

4. Gary Caldwell. *Les études ethniques au Québec — Bilan et perspectives.* Coll. « Instruments de travail » n° 8, 1983, 108 pages........................... 10,50 $

5. Honorius Provost. *Les premiers Anglo-Canadiens à Québec — Essai de recensement (1759-1775).* Coll. « Documents de recherche » n° 1, 2ᵉ édition, 1984, 71 pages.. 7,50 $

6. Tina Ioannou. *La communauté grecque du Québec.* Coll. « Identité et changements culturels » n° 4, 1984, 337 pages .... 18,00 $

7. Pierre Anctil et Gary Caldwell. *Juifs et réalités juives au Québec.* 1984, 371 pages .... 20,00 $

III   Chantier: La culture populaire

1. Yvan Lamonde, Lucia Ferretti et Daniel Leblanc. *La culture ouvrière à Montréal (1880-1920): bilan historiographique.* Coll. « Culture populaire » n° 1, 1982, 178 pages........................... 9,00 $

2. Danielle Nepveu. *Les représentations religieuses au Québec dans les manuels scolaires de niveau élémentaire (1950-1960).* Coll. « Documents préliminaires » n° 1, 1982, 97 pages....................... 6,50 $

3. Jean-Pierre Dupuis, Andrée Fortin, Gabriel Gagnon, Robert Laplante et Marcel Rioux. *Les pratiques émancipatoires en milieu populaire.* Coll. « Documents préliminaires » n° 2, 1982, 178 pages.. 9,00 $

4. Jean Bourassa. *Le travailleur minier, la culture et le savoir ouvrier.* Coll. « Documents préliminaires » n° 4, 1982, 79 pages...................................... 5,25 $

5. Sophie-Laurence Lamontagne. *L'hiver dans la culture québécoise (XVIIᵉ-XIXᵉ siècles).* 1983, 197 pages.. 11,50 $

6. Joseph Laliberté. *Agronome-colon en Abitibi.* Coll. « Littérature quotidienne » n° 1, 1983, 157 pages.. 12,00 $

7. Benoît Lacroix et Jean Simard. *Religion populaire, religion de clercs?* Coll. « Culture populaire » n° 2, 1984, 444 pages .... 22,00 $

8. Benoît Lacroix et Madeleine Grammond. *Religion populaire au Québec. Typologie des sources — Bibliographie sélective (1900-1980).* Coll. « Instruments de travail » n° 10, 1985, 175 pages....... 15,00 $

9. Andrée Fortin. *Le Rézo. Essai sur les coopératives d'alimentation au Québec.* Coll. « Documents de recherche » n° 5, 1985, 282 pages .... 17,00 $

IV Chantier: L'institutionnalisation de la culture

1. Jean-Robert Faucher, André Fournier et Gisèle Gallichan. *L'information culturelle dans les médias électroniques.* Coll. « Diagnostics culturels » n° 1, 1981, 167 pages .... 7,00 $

2. Angèle Dagenais. *Crise de croissance: le théâtre au Québec.* Coll. « Diagnostics culturels » n° 2, 1981, 73 pages... 5,00 $

3. Yvan Lamonde et Pierre-François Hébert. *Le cinéma au Québec — Essai de statistique historique (1896 à nos jours).* Coll. « Instruments de travail » n° 2, 1981, 481 pages........................ 18,00 $

4. François Colbert. *Le marché québécois du théâtre.* Coll. « Culture savante » n° 1, 1982, 112 pages

8,00 $

5. Jean-Pierre Charland et Nicole Thivierge. *Bibliographie de l'enseignement professionnel au Québec (1850-1980).* Coll. « Instruments de travail » n° 3, 1982, 284 pages .... 14,00 $

6. Vivian Labrie. *Précis de transcription de documents d'archives orales.* Coll. « Instruments de travail » n° 4, 1982, 220 pages .... 11,00 $

7. Sylvie Tellier. *Chronologie littéraire du Québec.* Coll. « Instruments de travail » n° 6, 1982, 352 pages... 18,50 $

8. Jean-Pierre Charland. *Histoire de l'enseignement technique et professionnel.* 1982, 485 pages......... 25,50 $

9. Nicole Thivierge. *Écoles ménagères et instituts familiaux: un modèle féminin traditionnel.* 1982, 478 pages... 25,50 $

10. Yvan Lamonde. *L'imprimé au Québec: aspects historiques (18ᵉ-20ᵉ siècles).* Coll. « Culture savante » nᵒ 2, 1983, 370 pages .... 18,00 $

11. Yvan Lamonde. *Je me souviens. La littérature personnelle au Québec (1860-1980).* Coll. « Instruments de travail » nᵒ 9, 1983, 278 pages......... 17,00 $

12. Claude Savary, dir. *Les rapports culturels entre le Québec et les États-Unis.* 1984, 353 pages......... 17,00 $

13. Pierre Lavoie. *Pour suivre le théâtre au Québec. Les ressources documentaires.* Coll. « Documents de recherche » nᵒ 4, 1985, 521 pages.... 22,00 $

14. Jacques Dufresne, Fernand Dumont et Yves Martin. *Traité d'anthropologie médicale. L'Institution de la santé et de la maladie.* Presses de l'Université du Québec, Institut québécois de recherche sur la culture, Presses Universitaires de Lyon, 1985, XVIII- 1 245 pages................. 49,95 $

V Chantier: Les régions du Québec

1. Jules Bélanger, Marc Desjardins et Yves Frenette. *Histoire de la Gaspésie.* Coll. « Les régions du Québec », Boréal Express, Montréal, 1981, 807 pages... 29,95 $

2. Jean-Claude Marsan. *Montréal, une esquisse du futur.* 1983, 325 pages............................. 15,00 $

3. André Dionne. *Bibliographie de l'île Jésus.* Coll. « Documents de recherche » nᵒ 2, 1983, 324 pages... 18,50 $

4. Serge Gauthier et collaborateurs. *Bibliographie de Charlevoix.* Coll. « Documents de recherche » nᵒ 3, 1984, 320 pages .... 18,00 $

5. Serge Gauthier et collaborateurs. *Guide des archives de Charlevoix.* 1985, VIII-97 pages.............. 6,00 $

VI Hors chantier

1. Paul Aubin. *Bibliographie de l'histoire du Québec et du Canada (1966-1975).* 2 tomes — 1981, 1 425 pages, 22 000 titres............................. 60,00 $

2. Gabrielle Lachance. *La culture contemporaine face aux industries culturelles et aux nouvelles technologies*. Rapport-synthèse, Rencontre franco-québécoise sur la culture, Québec-Montréal, du 4 au 8 juin 1984, 145 pages .... 7,00 $

3. *Statistiques culturelles du Québec, (1971-1982)*. 1985, XLII-932 pages .... 45,00 $

4. Paul Aubin et Louis-Marie Côté. *Bibliographie de l'histoire du Québec et du Canada/Bibliography of the History of Quebec and Canada (1976-1980)*. 2 tomes — 1985, LXIV-1 316 pages, 20 000 titres .... 60,00 $

VII « Questions de culture »

1. *Cette culture que l'on appelle savante*. 1981, 190 pages... 15,00 $

2. *Migrations et communautés culturelles*. 1982, 159 pages... 15,00 $

3. *Les cultures parallèles*. 1982, 172 pages .... 15,00 $

4. *Architectures: la culture dans l'espace*. 1983, 210 pages... 15,00 $

5. *Les régions culturelles*. 1983, 189 pages............. 12,00 $

6. *La culture et l'âge*. 1984, 198 pages .... 12,00 $

7. *La culture: une industrie?* 1984, 216 pages........ 12,00 $

8. *Présences de jeunes artistes*. 1985, 190 pages ...... 12,00 $

VIII Collection Edmond-de-Nevers

1. Lucie Robert. *Le manuel d'histoire de la littérature canadienne de Mgr Camille Roy*. 1982, 198 pages

11,00 $

2. Réal Brisson. *La charpenterie navale à Québec sous le régime français*. 1983, 320 pages.................. 19,50 $

3. Hélène Lafrance. *Yves Thériault et l'institution littéraire québécoise*. 1984, 174 pages................. 13,50 $

4. Hélène Laforce. *Histoire de la sage-femme dans la région de Québec*. 1985, 237 pages .... 19,50 $

IX Rapports de recherche et manuscrits à diffusion limitée*

1. Louise Rondeau. *Le récit de fin du monde: orientations méthodologiques de recherche.* Québec, IQRC, 1982, 70 pages.

2. Michelle Trudel-Drouin. *Vie quotidienne en Nouvelle-France: un choix de textes.* Montréal, IQRC, 1982, 166 pages.

3. Paule Chouinard. *Anthologie de poèmes québécois sur les saisons.* Montréal, IQRC, 1983, 1 350 pages.

4. Mireille Perreault. *Marchandisation, industrialisation de la culture.* Rimouski, IQRC, 1983, 72 pages.

5. Carmen Quintin. *Les pratiques émancipatoires dans deux coopératives d'habitation de la région montréalaise.* Montréal, IQRC, 1983, 124 pages.

6. Gary Caldwell, Paule Obermeir et al. *Outmigration of 1971 English Mother-tongue High School Leavers from Quebec: eleven years after.* Lennoxville, IQRC et Anglo Quebec en Mutation Committee, 1984, 37 pages.

X Banques de données sur support informatique

1. Jean-Pierre Chalifoux. *Le livre et la lecture au Québec au XX⁰ siècle.* Montréal, IQRC, 1982, (8 000 titres)**.

---

* disponibles sur demande à l'IQRC, 93, rue Saint-Pierre, Québec, G1K 4A3
(418) 643-4695.

** accessible sur demande à La Centrale des bibliothèques, 1685, rue Fleury est, Montréal, H2C 1T1
(514) 381-8891.

2. Paul Aubin et collaborateurs. *HISCABEQ. Biblio-graphie de l'histoire du Québec et du Canada (1946-1980)*. Montréal, IQRC, 1981, (57 000 titres — mise à jour trimestrielle)***.

XI Documents audio-visuels*

1. Arthur Lamothe. Culture amérindienne. Archives. (vingt documents produits par les Ateliers audio-visuels du Québec)

---

* disponibles sur demande à l'IQRC, 93, rue Saint-Pierre, Québec, G1K 4A3 (418) 643-4695.

*** pour s'abonner à HISCABEQ, communiquer avec IST-Informathèque Inc.
Service d'assistance technique:

Code régional	Numéro à composer
514	284-1100
418, 514, 613, 819	1-800-361-6165
416, 519, 705, 506, 902	1-800-361-7469

Achevé d'imprimer à Louiseville
sur les Presses de l'imprimerie Gagné ltée
en novembre mil neuf cent quatre-vingt-cinq